ALSO BY KAY ALLENBAUGH

Chocolate for a Woman's Soul

Chocolate for a Woman's Heart

Chocolate for a Lover's Heart

Chocolate for a Woman's Heart and Soul

INSPIRING STORIES

THAT CELEBRATE THE

SPIRIT OF MOTHERHOOD

A FIRESIDE BOOK
Published by Simon & Schuster

CHOCOLATE
for a
MOTHER'S
HEART

KAY ALLENBAUGH

FIRESIDE
Rockefeller Center
1230 Avenue of the Americas
New York, NY 10020

Copyright © 1999 by Kay Allenbaugh
All rights reserved,
including the right of reproduction
in whole or in part in any form.

FIRESIDE and colophon are registered trademarks
of Simon & Schuster Inc.

Manufactured in the United States of America

1 3 5 7 9 10 8 6 4 2

Library of Congress Cataloging-in-Publication Data is available.

ISBN 0-684-86299-9

With deep appreciation for our growing family,

I dedicate this book to the magnificence of:

David's unconditional generosity,

Rick's playful, wise being,

Peter's kind, thoughtful essence,

Tim's adventurous spirit,

Jenn's beautiful caring,

Stephanie's radiant light,

Amy's lovely innocence.

I love you all.

CONTENTS

III
THE INTUITIVE EDGE

IV
DIVINELY SENT

V
BETWEEN US GIRLS

VI
A MOTHER'S IMPRINT

VII

FAMILY FUNNIES

INTRODUCTION

*T*he inspirational stories you're about to read all deal with motherhood—you'll enjoy them whether you're a mom yourself or simply in need of a little mothering.

Moms have one of the simplest but toughest job descriptions around: Do it all, and then some! We're teachers, friends, chauffeurs, cooks, nurses, stage managers, career counselors, and most of all, safe havens. We need to know when to be there, and when to bite our tongues. We must shelter, guide, and protect—and then at precisely the right moment, push our precious offspring from the nest. Motherhood is a job with more variety than the biggest box of chocolates you can envision! And that's why all the stories in *Chocolate for a Mother's Heart* were written with so many different types of women in mind.

Of course, you don't need to be a mom or need some mothering to understand the double-edged nature of the maternal instinct—women who have a motherly nature always seem to be the ones others depend upon, whether it's at home or in the office, whether it's a child who needs some mothering, a spouse, a best friend, or even our own moms! And because all mothers seem to hold themselves up to such high standards, sometimes they need a little extra nurturing—and indulging—too. That's why the stories in this new "chocolate" book were written to inspire, empower, and delight you.

Chocolate for a Mother's Heart is an extension of my journey after being divinely inspired to write *Chocolate for a Woman's Soul*.

My own mother died young, at age forty, when I was fifteen years old. The enormous loss I've felt over the years has been a constant reminder to me of how irreplaceable mothers really are. But though I miss my mother, I know that she's always been with me in spirit, protecting me as I go through life. Losing Mom has also made me incredibly grateful for all the time I've been given with my children.

With the kind of unconditional love that only a mother can provide—and a reminder that mothers know best—I offer you a variety of deliciously rich, real-life "chocolate stories." So go ahead, indulge in these soul-satisfying treats, and take it from this mom: they will just whet your appetite for more!

I
MILK AND COOKIES

*"The journey toward the heart
is always a journey home."*

—JENNIFER JAMES, Ph.D.

"A child does not thrive on what [she] is prevented from doing,
but on what [she] actually does."
—MARCELENE COX

A DIFFERENT PERSPECTIVE

W hen my daughter Adrienne was twelve years old, she took a photography class. She informed me that real photographers use black-and-white film. I agreed. We bought the film and she decided to take pictures of the St. Louis Gateway Arch.

The day was overcast. I recommended we wait for sun, but she thought the light optimal for the photograph she envisioned. The minute we got to the arch, Adrienne walked up to one of the massive triangular-shaped legs, arched her entire body backwards against it, arms stretched overhead, and pointed her camera straight up the side.

I said in my most caring, motherly voice, "Honey, you need to back up and get the entire arch in the picture." Anyone who has ever seen a photo of the arch knows what I mean. "It won't make sense if you can't see the entire thing," I said.

She ignored me and moved to the other leg, repeating her position. I tried again to tell her the best way to take the picture. I wanted her to get a good photograph, but she was clearly unimpressed by my sage advice and years of experience snapping birthday parties, dance recitals, and vacations.

"No, I want to do it this way," she said.

I thought, okay, we'll waste a little money on film and developing, but she'll learn her lesson.

It turns out I learned the lesson. Years later, Adrienne won a scholarship from the San Francisco Art Institute, interned at Ansel Adams Center for Photography, and had a show at the Museum of Modern Art in San Francisco. People buy her photographs because she has a unique vision. A vision that spurred her at twelve to photograph the Gateway Arch from an angle I thought would never work.

The way my daughter approached that photo taught this mother that most solutions we need are right in front of us—if we are willing to look at an opportunity with a new and different perspective.

Thank goodness Adrienne didn't see the arch through my lens. That photo has been purchased by collectors and now hangs in several galleries.

LINDA NASH

"We are rich only through what we give,
and poor only through what we refuse."
—ANNE-SOPHIE SWETCHINE

THE RARE MONGOLIAN RABBIT

*P*erhaps the frequency with which it so often happens nowadays should have lessened the pain; misery does love company, after all. But hearing that my husband's job would be "phased out" was unforgettable and shocking.

John, my husband of ten years, expressed his concern over this nightmare occurrence. He assured me that he would do everything possible to get a job to provide for our family. With three children under the age of five and one due very shortly, we relied on his income entirely.

"Life goes on," John said, more outwardly upbeat than I over the situation. "We have our health, and after all, it's only a job. Besides, the company will continue paying me for three more months. I'll surely have a new job by then. Just relax and don't worry."

With his excellent university and professional credentials, I figured he must be right. He was a former Olympic athlete and knew about taking on a challenge. His father died when John was young, so he took on the responsibility of keeping his mother, sister, and brother together. My husband knew how to work hard and smart. But as the months passed and no job possibilities materialized for him, I grew more and more fearful and less "faith-abiding." What if he couldn't find a job? Under other circumstances I could have returned to classroom teaching, but our fourth child was due in less than three months.

With little money in our savings account, the mortgage payment two months behind, and no possible income from any other source, I whittled away at our daily-living budget.

Eventually our food budget became almost nonexistent. One day while in the supermarket with my children, I noticed a young box boy packing overly ripe fruit and outdated food into cardboard boxes. Hesitantly, I inquired about the destination of the food. "We sell it real cheap, and whatever isn't sold is thrown away," he said. I eyed the aging carrots, celery, tomatoes. Food we could use for weeks. What, I wondered, is the proper etiquette for begging for food for one's children?

"We have a rare Mongolian rabbit!" I heard myself blurt out, glancing at my three hungry children. "I'd be interested in purchasing the food for the rabbit."

He replied easily, "Since it's just a rabbit, there won't be any charge."

That day he loaded five boxes of produce into my car. We talked while he worked, me sharing information about my soon-to-be-expanding family and him talking about his. His name was Jeff. I learned he came from a family of five where finances were tight. This job helped pay for his college education.

Weeks went by, and Jeff began packing the boxes with outdated or damaged items—peanut butter, soup, and cheese—that were otherwise still good but would be thrown away. "Surely a rare rabbit would eat all these items," he said, explaining their inclusion. As the weeks turned into months, we discovered, hidden under the produce, laundry detergent, milk, juice, butter . . . the list goes on and on. Jeff started phoning me every time he had a box of "rabbit food" ready. Now and then, he brought the boxes to our home. He never inquired after the rabbit, content instead to leave its food and be on his way.

When our fourth daughter was born, my elation was tinged with worry about our financial future. "O Lord, please," I begged. "You promised you would never give us more than we can handle. What do you want us to do? Help!"

My husband slipped into the hospital room and said, "I have good news and sad news. The good news is that this morning I've been offered a very exciting job." I closed my eyes and thanked God for his many blessings. "The sad news," he continued, "is that the rare Mongolian rabbit is gone."

It turned out Jeff no longer worked at the supermarket. While I'd been busy with the birth of our new baby, he had moved, the manager said, and left no forwarding address.

Over the next ten years I made good on my silent promise to repay the kindness of all who had helped us throughout that difficult time. But my thanks were incomplete. Then one day, a decade later, there was Jeff standing in the store's office. I noticed the title MANAGER on his name badge.

How does one adequately thank the person who offers assistance without compromising your pride, extends a hand without sapping your strength, and believes in the rare Mongolian rabbits hiding somewhere in each of our lives? I'm not surprised Jeff's risen up the ranks. He has a rare gift. He knew how to listen loudly to my special plea.

"Mrs. Nunn!" he exclaimed, "I think of you and your family often. How is the rabbit?" he inquired softly.

Taking Jeff's hands into mine, I whispered with a wink, "Thanks for asking. The rabbit moved on long ago, and we couldn't be better."

MAUREEN NUNN

ADVENTURES IN GRANDPARENTING

I *had a date with my five-year-old grandson to do some* spring skiing in the California mountains at Bear Lake. I couldn't wait to wrap my arms around that boy and look into his smiling eyes. I'd taken him on his inaugural ski adventure some months before. He had hung on to that tow rope for dear life, and then spent most of his time bouncing and sliding his way down the bunny hill. No matter how he got to the bottom, once there he would throw his arms up to the sky in jubilation. I remember saying to him, "Justin, what I like best about you is that you don't give up!"

Before flying to California for our next special time together, I introduced Justin to the notion that you can "set an intention" for just about anything you want to do, and make it happen in spite of the obstacles. After talking on the phone several times before the trip, we decided on our intention: To have a fun and grand adventure together—no matter what. I told him to picture that in his mind over and over again, and I would do the same.

I picked him up on a glorious sunny morning. "You know, there's just one possible little snag that we need to talk about," I said to Justin as we started our drive toward the mountain. "Last night, El Niño blew through and dumped eight inches of fresh powder on these mountains. The ski conditions are going to be great, but the road conditions might be tricky. There might be too much ice and snow on the road for this rental car to make it, because I don't have any chains."

True, we didn't have chains, and I didn't want to buy any. Why buy chains when I've never ever successfully put chains on a car? Justin turned to me, gave me his big, knowing smile, and said, "Let's go, Grandma!" So onward we climbed, gradually making our way up the mountain pass. We came around a bend, and the first challenge to our intention confronted us. Ice! Not just a little patch, but ice on the road as far as you could see.

Eight cars had pulled over, and a body was sticking out from below each one as these drivers attempted to put on their chains. Friends and family offered encouragement and advice to those contorted under their cars. Not a pretty sight. I found myself thinking quickly about alternative ways to entertain Justin.

"Well, Justin," I said, "this may be a challenge for us." Just as I was about to say, "Hey, how about we turn back and go see a movie instead?" Justin piped up. "You know, Grandma, what I like best about us is that we don't give up." Why did that sound so familiar? We were definitely at a decision point when I remembered that the intention of this trip was to be an adventure. And *anything* can happen on an adventure.

Buoyed by his confidence, I turned back to the market we had passed ten miles back to see if they had chains. Still feeling a need to point out the practical side of things, I said, "Now, there's no guarantee that they will have any chains, and there's no guarantee that I'm going to be able to get them on the car. I've never been able to do it before." Justin responded simply, "Let's go see, and then we'll ask God for help." He put his hands together, and with all the faith in his tiny body, he prayed, "Dear God, please help my grandma put on the chains, and if she can't, send a man." What a great idea! My excitement mounted as we confronted the second challenge to our intention of having a grand adventure together—no matter what.

With lightning speed, the guy at the market sold us chains to fit the rental car, and we were back on the road. Approaching the familiar icy curve, I slowed down, ready to pull in behind a line of cars like the one we'd seen on our first attempt up the mountain. As we rounded the bend, no one was there. Lots of ice, but not a car to be seen.

My heart sank as the third challenge to having a great adventure presented itself. Once again, Justin focused on our goal as I focused on the obstacles. Just as I was about to prepare my grandson for the inevitable, he said it again: "The thing I like best about us, Grandma, is that we don't give up." So, of course, I had to give it a shot. And I did. And I failed. *Time to go home and find a movie,* I said to myself as I struggled fruitlessly with the heavy chains. Then, I heard a voice say, "Ma'am, can I help you?" I turned around and faced a John Wayne look-alike. Moments later, with chains in place, we were on our way again.

Several miles later, I heard the unmistakable thud of chains coming undone. It seemed like the forces were against us as the fourth challenge to our intention surfaced—before we'd even reached the ski slopes. Fresh out of ideas, I muttered under my breath, "Set an intention, picture it over and over—no matter what." Within moments of my pulling over, a man stopped his pickup, hopped out, grabbed his tools, and tightened the chains. I didn't even need to ask him for assistance. Maybe the Force was with us after all.

The day became one Disney moment after another. The hills were alive with the sound of music as we sang "Banana, bo-bana" while racing down the slopes. The brook was babbling. The sun was shining and Justin was skiing powder—a grand adventure—just as we intended!

Exhausted and exhilarated at the end of a glorious day, we loaded our skis and boots back into the car and I slid behind the wheel. My grandson, this five-year-old bundle of joy seated next to me, looked up at me with his radiant eyes. Confidently he said, "Grandma, you know what I like best about us?"

REV. MARY OMWAKE

FAMILY SCENTS

My Aunt Esther loved children, all of them. When she realized she would never have a child of her own, she wisely followed her heart and became a teacher. Outside the classroom, when she wasn't gardening or canning, she entertained and taught the other children in her life. Fortunately, my sister and I were among the lucky ones.

We adored her, and why not? She let us do darn near anything. We could turn any room into a fort, build a seawall in the bathtub, or create weird science experiments in the kitchen. She played the part of the ringmaster as our imaginations ran wild! I remember her as magical, perhaps partly because of the way she smelled. She favored a pine-scented soap that seemed to permeate the air with a hint of tingling, almost mystical energy.

I admit I failed to recognize her real gifts until I grew older. In reflection, I imagine the true beauty of my aunt's spirit came from her refusal to use the word "mistake" or "failure" in the presence of a child. In her eyes we could do anything or become anyone, and because of that belief in us, many times we did!

Years later, my sister and I had our own children, and they too got to experience the "magic" of a visit to Aunt Esther's house. As babies, each one of the six children sat in her sunny dining nook and tried to catch sunbeams as they streamed in from a window smudged with handprints. Regardless of how many children she'd witnessed do the same, she always exclaimed, "Now, that's a remarkable child. Look, he's [or she's] already fascinated with the mystery of nature."

I think the weekend one of the girls pretended to be a "doggy" best illustrates this kind woman's patience and willingness to encourage imagination. Little Jennifer spent three days running around the house on her hands and knees. Barely speaking, she chose instead to bark or whine her needs to Aunt Esther. "Why, she even allowed her to eat out of dishes on the floor," my father remarked with a shake of his head.

Throughout the years, she taught generations of children everything from the joy of feeding ducks in the front-yard ponds to the more refined appreciation of literature. I'll always treasure the rainy afternoons we spent in her living room listening to her read from a poetry book or one of the classics.

When she died, she left us quietly, with dignity and grace. We were all comforted by the knowledge that she spent her final days surrounded by family and friends. It served as a fitting farewell to a woman who gave so much.

Considering all the wondrous moments she created on earth, it shouldn't come as a surprise to learn she still works her magic from beyond. A few sensitive souls in my family get an occasional visit from Aunt Esther; we call them "scentings."

I'll never forget the day my sister called to tell me about "the most amazing thing that just happened." She'd smelled the unmistakable scent of our aunt's soap and noticed an indentation on a freshly made bed. A bed that once belonged to Aunt Esther. In addition, my sister says, she was overcome with feelings of peace and love.

A couple of the older kids, the ones who once played at her feet years ago, also tell stories of awakening from a fitful sleep to a scent of pine and a feeling that their great-aunt is watching over them. Even my mother has experienced a "scenting" or two. "Especially," she says, "when I'm mulling over an issue or worried about one of the children." It's no accident, I'm sure, that my aunt visits when one of us is in need of a little extra faith or love.

Many evenings, I sit in quiet solitude and think of her. There's little sadness in remembering, since all my memories of her fill my heart with smiles and joy. Every now and again, in the still night air, she sits with me. I sense the tingle and smell the pine, while I imagine the lined and loving face of the woman who wore it well.

DEBB JANES

A LONG WAY FROM HOME

The year was 1947. My parents loaded the car with suitcases while I looked for my elusive tomcat, Snoonie, to say goodbye. I was excited to be vacationing in my favorite place in the whole world—Atlantic City: cotton candy, saltwater taffy, the steel pier, the beach, and all the ocean a ten-year-old could want.

Calling for him, I entered the woods behind my house to search the wild apple orchard and his blackberry patch hideout. I never figured out why we chose that name for a cat. A family epithet, I was told. No matter. I loved him, and I knew in cat language that he loved me. I had no siblings, and Snoonie was my tolerant confidant. I told him everything.

Sure enough, he sauntered out from under a ripe berry bush, stretching and mewing at me for having disturbed his summer nap. I cradled him in my arms and said, "Time to go on vacation, but you have to stay here. I wish you could come with me, but they don't allow cats or dogs at the motel." I scratched between his ears until I heard his soft, rhythmic purr and whispered, "Be good for Janet and her mom. And no leaving mice at their front door with the morning paper. And don't beg food from the men building the house across the street." I kissed the little black circle atop Snoonie's head. "See you in three weeks," I said, and situated him beneath the bush again.

It was early September when we returned from Atlantic City. I jumped from the car and began calling for Snoonie. I combed the woods, shouting his name. There was no sign of him. An ominous feeling was growing in the pit of my stomach as I raced to my friend Janet's house, only to discover my beloved cat had been missing for a week. Janet and her mother had checked the entire neighborhood, while keeping bowls of fresh cat food at the door. I pushed the horror of squished road cats from my mind and kept telling myself that Snoonie would turn up.

One afternoon a workman from the crew across the street waved me over.

"Little girl," he said, "I hear you calling for Snoonie every day. Is that a dog or a cat, or what?"

"It's my cat. He's a black-and-white boy cat with a circle atop his head. We left on vacation for three weeks, and now he's gone." I tried to hold back welling tears, but they overflowed and ran down my cheeks.

The workman removed his cap and scratched his head, thinking. "Black and white, you say. Yeah, there was a cat like that hanging around here. One of the guys used to feed him tuna from his lunch box. When his plumbing job was over, and no one had claimed the cat, he thought it was a stray and took it home with him."

"Where does he live?" I exclaimed with relief. "I'll tell my dad and we'll drive to the man's house and get Snoonie back."

"I can't help you there, little girl," the workman said, shaking his head. "All I know is the man's name is Frank and he lives in the city—miles away from here."

I went home crying. My parents questioned the workman again, even called the contractor supervising the job, but he didn't have any information on Frank. Then they sat me down to tell me the words I didn't want to hear—my Snoonie was gone. "We'll get you another kitty," my mother said in an attempt to cheer me up. I didn't want another cat. I wanted Snoonie back.

When winter had blanketed our house with snow that fell hard and heavy, I would sit on the sofa overlooking the window-sill where Snoonie used to perch. Though he wasn't with me, I remembered him in my prayers, asking God to please bring him back.

One unforgettable night, while on the sofa, I saw a flicker of movement. I glanced out at the sill and saw a very bedraggled and scrawny black-and-white cat. I started yelling, "Snoonie! Snoonie!" Somehow, my brave cat had come home to his family. We were overjoyed to see him and immediately set out to fatten him up.

Days later, there was a knock at our door. It was a stranger, a man who introduced himself as Frank. My father invited him in. Frank said he had run into the contractor and heard our story. Then he apologized for taking our cat home with him. He said he would have returned the cat, but that Snoonie was now missing from his house and he was afraid the cat had been run over by busy traffic. My dad laughed and said, "Wait until you see this!" He took Frank to the dining room heating vent, where Snoonie was curled up sleeping on his blanket.

"I can't believe my eyes," Frank said, bending down to scratch Snoonie's black circle. We told him the date our cat had returned and how emaciated he looked. "It's a miracle," Frank remarked. "I figure he was traveling for about two months. I live in the city, some thirty-five miles from here." He smiled down at my contented, purring cat and said, "I guess he took the long way home."

JOAN ROELKE

BABY MARK

y *son-in-law and I had spent three restless days* in my daughter's 12-foot-by-12-foot labor room. Shortly before midnight her doctor gave up on a natural delivery and prepared us for a cesarean birth. When I asked if I might still be able to see my grandchild come into the world, I was told that there was only room for the father in the surgical suite. The doctor encouraged my son-in-law to take a quick break while they prepared my daughter for surgery. He did so, but on his way back to the suite, the elevator he rode in became stuck between floors! The nurses dressed me instead to go into the operating room.

I arrived just as the doctor made the incision in my daughter's belly. I took a seat beside her head. She was sedated yet fully conscious, and her disappointment that her husband wasn't there soothing her between contractions was understandable.

As the nurse held the baby up for my daughter to see, he turned from a pink-tinted blue to gray. His little head flopped over. Heartache and pain overwhelmed me, but I managed to keep stroking my daughter's head, telling her about the baby's long black hair and how beautiful he looked. The nurse confirmed my fears when I heard her say, "Breathe, baby, breathe." My daughter's breath quickened, and she stretched to see past the sheet draped to block our view.

"Your baby is very sick," the nurse said as she scooped my grandson up and ran for the back corridor leading into the intensive care unit. Halfway down the corridor she turned, looked at me and said, "Are you coming?" Me in ICU? Absolutely not. The ache in my heart weighted me to the plastic orange chair. I couldn't bear to bond with this child knowing he might not live. I turned to my daughter. "Do you want me to go with the baby?" She sank back into the bed, closed her eyes, and nodded yes.

Three doctors and six nurses worked on my grandson in the ICU. They motioned me to come near, but I refused. As this newborn clung to life on a ventilator, nurses inserted more tubes and lovingly patted him. "Come on, baby," they said. "Come on."

Finally something inside me burst. "His name is *Mark!*" I shouted. The staff paused and looked at me. I felt as small as the baby. Monitors ticked, whirred, and bleeped. "Keep moving," someone said, and their frenetic pace resumed. Early in her pregnancy, I remembered my daughter mentioning six names, including Mark. Nurses wrote "Mark" on all my grandson's instruments, and it cemented my connection with him that I knew I wouldn't lose no matter what.

With as much compassion as possible, the doctors gave me a blow-by-blow prognosis. Mark's lungs were filled with fluid, he couldn't breathe on his own, they suspected heart problems and the possibility of spinal meningitis. "Pray," a doctor told me. Although I have always loved God, I didn't hold much hope after the doctors' diagnosis. I'd known of many mothers and grandmothers who'd prayed their most sincere prayers, only to lose their babies.

With my son-in-law now at my daughter's side, they wheeled her bed into the ICU, and the doctors repeated the prognosis. She turned to me and said, "Mom, he's going to be okay, isn't he?" I'd always made everything okay for my daughter, and she needed to hear me say he would be all right, but I couldn't lie. Although my response was noncommittal, I tried to reassure her.

Moments later, out of nowhere, my daughter sat straight up and with great conviction and passion called out, "Mom, he's going to make it! I know he is!" She described a loving presence in the room that surrounded her and suddenly embraced me as well. We both knew this dear baby would be fine.

Within a few hours, my grandson began breathing on his own. Each time I left my daughter's room to check on him, another tube had been removed. He drank his first feeding in two gulps, and his doctor had to be consulted to see if he could have another bottle. A nurse came to announce the good news. "Mark has stabilized," she told us with a big smile.

Oops . . . I realized in all the excitement, I forgot to tell her! My daughter, with a puzzled look on her face, turned to the nurse and asked, "Who's *Mark?*"

JUDITH MCCLURE

A BOUNTIFUL HARVEST

*W*hen our first daughter arrived, I didn't hesitate a minute to leave a successful business career to devote myself full-time to making a warm, loving home for our new family. As the years moved on, I never regretted that decision. I genuinely enjoyed my life as a wife, homemaker, and mother. Besides the obvious warm fuzzies of creating a satisfying marriage and cuddling the babies, home life held additional rewards for me. I became an accomplished painter, plasterer, carpenter, and fix-it handyperson. Repeated relocations, due to my husband's career, transformed me into an expert packer and expediter. My artistic talents emerged as I sewed clothes for the children and accessorized one home after another.

Fifteen years later, the life course I had chosen took an abrupt about-face when I had to return to the business world and recreate my ability to earn a living outside the home. Despite long-term counseling, communication with my husband had evaporated and our marriage crumbled. Our lives, headed in different directions, resulted in a long-drawn-out and very difficult divorce.

Not quite fully recovered from the divorce, I struggled terribly with the demands of being a single parent of three active children. Two teenagers and a nine-year-old managed to keep me forever working. Stretching available funds to extraordinary lengths became a daily contest. Haunted by guilt, I watched the children do without so much because I just couldn't afford the extras anymore.

To provide sufficient one-on-one time and moral support for each of the children became my most difficult challenge as a single parent. Time conflicts were all too common. My cheerfulness, energy, and self-esteem eroded daily. Although I had always been a loving, nurturing parent, I started second-guessing my parenting abilities: Am I being too strict, too lenient? Am I giving each child enough attention? Am I setting a good example? Most important, are the children learning the values I want so much to impart to them? Do they feel my love? I felt like a failure.

My oldest daughter, usually a very quiet and private teen, had joined the drama club at school and started acting. This new aspect of her personality surprised and delighted me. The night of her premiere performance, I sat in the front row. Unable to afford roses from a florist, I made her a lovely bouquet of mixed flowers tied together with a rainbow of ribbons.

When the play ended and the cast lined up across the stage for their initial bows, my son ran up and handed his sister the flowers. She positively glowed with happiness and excitement. Yet when the curtains closed and then reopened for the cast's individual bows, she reappeared without the bouquet. I convinced myself that she was disappointed she hadn't received roses as some of the other actresses had. Feeling I'd let her down one more time, tears filled my eyes. Then I noticed that the supporting actresses all appeared with small bunches of flowers cradled in their arms. Now the tears really streamed down my cheeks as I realized my daughter had broken apart her bouquet so that all her friends had flowers to carry on stage for the final applause.

In one wonderful moment, her small act of kindness—like magic—provided the affirmation my sagging spirit needed. She had learned to do more with less. She had come through the pain of divorce okay. So would her brother and sister. And so would I.

Patricia Kulzer

THELMA SAVES LOUISE

I simply didn't want to adopt two little fur balls. It had only been seven weeks since Shauna, my tortoiseshell cat, my wonderful friend and companion, died. For seventeen years she had comforted me through life's ups and downs with no judgment. That cat knew all my secrets and never told anyone. She loved me unconditionally, and I her.

I rescued her from an animal shelter in Green Bay, Wisconsin. The moment I picked her up, I knew she belonged with me. She put one paw around each side of my neck, buried her head into me, and purred. I'm really not sure who picked whom. While I was still grieving that huge loss, my friend Linda showed up at my door with two kittens. "They have nowhere else to go! Look at their cute little faces. Please, you have to save them, Joanne." I felt torn, not ready for a new cat—let alone two—yet agreeing halfheartedly that I would take them in.

I woke up the next morning to two frisky little beings jumping all over me, wide-eyed, wondering why I didn't hurry up and play with them. I flashed on Shauna, who right about now would have been curled up at my side, wondering why I didn't just go back to sleep. I looked right in the faces of these two creatures, knowing we were destined to spend years together and questioned, *How did this happen? And who are you two?*

It didn't take long for those magical bonds to form. I named these feisty critters Thelma and Louise. They'd never take the place of Shauna, but they both wormed their way deeper and deeper into my heart until I couldn't imagine life without them.

Early one morning about six months later, I gathered my things together, ready to head to work. I said goodbye to Louise and turned to say goodbye to Thelma when I noticed her behaving very strangely. I walked into the kitchen to take a closer look. She was in the corner meowing, jumping up and down, and batting at something on the wall. I had never seen her act this way before. "Thelma, what are you doing?" She ignored me and continued to meow and bat at the wall. I looked at where she was hitting and felt the surface. Hotter than an iron! Red hot! I slid my hand up the wall and as I got near the outlet, my hand started to burn. *A fire! Oh, my God! There's a fire in the wall!*

Five minutes later, two firemen were swinging an ax through my kitchen wall, putting out an electrical fire that had started in the wiring. I kept looking over at Thelma thinking, *How did you know?*

Afterward, one of the firemen looked at me and said, "It's a good thing you called when you did. If you had left for work, I'm afraid your house would no longer be standing here."

After he left, I just stood there, holding my two kitties and looking at the hole in the wall. I kissed Thelma again and again and told her what a good cat she'd been. Too busy for words of praise, she jumped from my arms and immediately became enthralled with an emery board she found on the floor, flipping it in the air, grabbing it, carrying it in her mouth as if she were a lioness with her prey.

Both she and Louise like to snuggle up and lick me at the end of the day. Both have earned a great big place in my heart, right along with Shauna.

When I finally did go into work, news of my tale spread like wildfire (pardon the pun). Everyone knew Thelma was a hero. Later that day I checked my mailbox and found that one of my coworkers had dropped off a cartoon. It showed a jet plane about to go down in flames with a poodle at the wheel. "FiFi saves the day!"

Being our savior hasn't gone to Thelma's head. She continues to attack emery boards, likes to walk along the edge of the bathtub—only occasionally falling in—and attacks my toes when I move them under the covers.

I thought I'd saved them by taking them in, but in reality— they saved me.

JOANNE MCCALL

II
MOMS KNOW BEST

"Biology is the least of what makes someone a mother."

—Oprah Winfrey

THE TIES THAT BIND

When our son, Rick, told us he planned to marry Amy, my husband and I were ecstatic. A playful, loving couple in their twenties, these two rock-and-roll musicians could not have had more in common—including two doting mothers.

With the wedding a year away, we combined resources with Amy's mom so that the two young lovers might have their perfect wedding.

Weddings call for all the important people in the bride and groom's life to be present. Although both of them are high-functioning beings in the world, they also carry unwanted baggage. Family life and logistics are complicated for kids of divorce.

Rick's dad had left fifteen years before, moving to another state to marry the "other" woman. I married Eric four years later. Rick's feelings of abandonment because his dad simply wasn't around fueled a continual guilty reaction from his father, who claimed all Rick wanted when they talked was money. Infrequent contact over the years punctuated a wilted relationship. Amy's dad was an absentee parent altogether. Although he lived in the same city, she had not seen her father in fourteen years, but she yearned to be loved by him.

Amy worked up the courage to write her dad a letter about six months before the wedding. She introduced herself, told him who she had become, and welcomed his response. He wrote back praising her accomplishments but did not suggest they get together.

The bride-to-be personally designed and engraved her wedding invitations and sent one to her father as well. Rick's dad responded that he wouldn't be attending because his name was not included on the invitation. Rick was disappointed but not really surprised. Amy came home from work one day and was overcome with emotion by the voice she heard on her answering machine. "Amy, this is your dad. I'd be honored to be at your wedding." Another reminder of the lopsided world of divorce.

We rented out the bed-and-breakfast for a day and a half. The wedding ceremony would take place in the living area and the bride and groom, aunts, uncles, sisters, and brothers could stay the night in the rooms upstairs. The majestic historic landmark with its period furniture, rich mahogany moldings, butter-yellow living room, and bronze and crystal chandeliers set the stage for Amy's elegant taste to emerge. To offset her ivory gown, Amy asked the groomsmen to wear dark suits, and her attendants to each wear a long, black dress of their choice. Berries, dried hydrangeas, and fall leaves were secured together by copper-colored ribbons for the exquisite bouquets.

Trees showed off their fall colors on the crisp, sunny wedding day. The front door of the bed-and-breakfast was swung wide open so that guests could file in easily. I recognized Amy's dad immediately from how her mom had described him. I knew that Amy longed to be escorted by her father from the dressing room along the outside walkway of the bed-and-breakfast up to the porch, where she would make a grand entrance through the front door. With her mom's blessing, I asked him. He seemed nervous but anxious to please.

When the beautiful bride and her dad walked into the foyer, she stopped and nuzzled his neck before letting go of his arm. She then walked toward Rick and took a few short inhales—more like audible sobs from a bride on emotional overload.

All was not serious at this wedding, however. Rick and Amy wanted to choose who would perform the ceremony. They didn't want to have a particular religious denomination repre-sented, so they selected a clergyman who had received his cre-dentials from a mail-order ad in *Rolling Stone*. At the wedding, the general consensus was that the minister's lights were not on. Our suspicions were confirmed when, at the end of the ceremony, he introduced the newlyweds as "Mrs. and Mrs." Rick Bain.

When Amy's mom graciously allowed Amy's dad to play an important part in the ceremony, and he rose to the occasion, Amy was allowed to heal a lifetime of hurts. When Rick was able to let go of his wish that his father be present, he was able to focus on the hundred people present who loved him and wished them well. They created and pulled off their perfect wedding in an imperfect world.

After a lively reception, followed by dinner, the bride and groom decided to call it a night and they headed to their room. About ten minutes later, Amy's mom and I got word from the innkeeper that the bride and groom wanted to say good night. So we knocked gently at their door and walked into the bridal suite, dimly lit by antique lamps.

The newlyweds, wrapped up in white terry-cloth bathrobes provided by the bed-and-breakfast, were lying under the covers, grinning from ear to ear. In their eyes, we saw another opportu-nity for love and happiness to blossom.

Like two mother bears, bound by our devotion to our cubs, we walked to the head of the bed, leaned over and tucked our kids in, then symbolically traded sides and tucked again—forever sealing those ties that bind.

KAY ALLENBAUGH

SAM'S PURPOSE

For years now, I have held the hands of the dying. "How can you bear it?" people ask me. "Hospice nursing must be so difficult. How can you stand to be around so much suffering?" Those people don't understand that if you have the courage to look beyond suffering, you find strength. If you have the forbearance to tackle deformity, you encounter triumph. I know this for a fact. Sam taught me.

An unlikely teacher, this infant of mine. The one the pediatrician said I couldn't take home from the hospital after his birth. Disappointment had struck me then, as a new twenty-year-old mother, but fear lodged in me when the doctor mentioned serious problems and the need for more tests. Shock and disbelief gripped me when he predicted Sam would not improve. When I found a small voice to ask what we could do now, he seemed almost irritated at my lack of comprehension. As if to settle the matter once and for all, he blurted, "Your baby is severely retarded. He will probably never roll over, never sit, never crawl, never walk or talk." Then, returning to an attempt at advising with compassion, he said, "You're young and healthy. You can have more children. You should begin to think of institutional placement for him." I stopped listening, turned, and walked a few feet toward my hospital bed. I pulled the curtain between me and the world and began to cry as quietly as I could. I looked at the waiting baby layette beside me and began to sob harder.

For the first week I returned every day to stand and stare silently through the nursery window, longing to hold and comfort that baby and myself. Afterward I left and cried for hours more. I woke up every night ready to shake the nightmare, only to feel the more helpless reality. But by the beginning of the second week, I began to feel myself steeling. I stopped crying and did not cry about anything for a very long time. Sam needed me.

My little boy, stricken with cerebral palsy and severe sight and hearing impairments, came home to me after one month. Sam's life has not passed easily. Crayons never seemed a natural fit in his hand. The sound of the ice cream truck never reached his ears to cheer him on a summer day. No one ever chose him to play on the kickball teams hastily thrown together in the street by the neighborhood kids. Yet he has triumphed over every one of the predictions, the imposed limitations dropped upon him by a medical community lacking faith in the spirit of one small boy. With countless hours of therapy sessions, love, encouragement—and mostly his own unbelievable motivation—he learned to speak, read, write, and at age nine walk on his own. And interestingly, as Sam learned to walk, I discovered my independence. As he learned to speak, I too found my voice. The first time he made a joke and a stranger laughed heartily, I discovered the unblemished joy of a life—any life!—well lived.

Because of Sam, I needed to hurry to find the spirited person within myself that I had never seen before. That kind of purpose and spirit has carried me through a humiliating divorce, a number of moves, college, and a career in hospice nursing. It has given me the courage to change my life from one of sterile comfort to one of rich love. Sam needed someone to respond, stand, and speak for him. He needed someone to begin to turn the world right side up again.

That day in the nursery, thirty-three years ago, I knew that he trusted me to do it, so I became that person. With my baby's support, I became the mother he needed. In the process, I also became the woman I always wanted to be.

LINDA RAY

"My mother phones daily to ask, 'Did you just try to reach me?'
When I reply, 'No,' she adds, 'So, if you're not too busy,
call me while I'm still alive,' and hangs up."
—ERMA BOMBECK

DEAREST LAST-BORN

On May 2, 1926, my parents got married, a condition in which they remained for over sixty-seven years. For the last fifteen of those years, they spent six months a year arguing in Florida and six months a year arguing in New York. During the Florida phase, my mother loved for me to write to her, but because of my busy travel and lecture schedule, I'm rarely in a position to do that, since it's impossible to write and drive at the same time. Therefore, I usually call her on the phone. This is the response to one of my phone calls:

> *Dearest Sweetheart,*
> *It was a pleasure hearing your voice, but your letters give me a bigger thrill, because I read and re-read them. I'm looking forward to seeing you and the kids. How are they doing in school and at home? The movie sounded interesting. Where did you eat? We love you very much. Kiss the kids for us.*
>
> *Just Dad and Me*

Now I ask you, is that a humble person? "Just Dad and Me." That's like getting an eviction notice signed "Just the Landlord."

In any event, how could I deprive my wonderful mother of a letter for her to read and reread? So I wrote her a letter, and here is her response:

> *Dearest Last born,*
>
> *It's really a marvelous thing for a daughter to get a minute's time to write after a two month vacation. I can't understand what you are doing at the senior citizen's. What do you teach them? At this stage of life, I would think you could take lessons from them! I'm glad you had that article to send me, otherwise I don't think I would even have gotten the letter yet. Anyway, I love you and I'm happy to hear that you are enjoying life. Please, please continue! Give my kids a big hug and kiss for me.*
>
> *Love from Dad and Me*

Well, now I decided I could write her a long letter, which I did. I called to tell her I had just sent her the longest letter I had ever written, and she was never going to complain again. Right? Wrong! Here is the answer to my longest letter:

> *Dear Joyce,*
>
> *Yes, your letter was a nice long one. But a letter is a letter, and you only used one stamp, so that means it is only one letter. Come on kid, you will have to write again, and soon. Trying to get you on the phone is a great big joke. Do you ever get off? I have tried a half dozen times and the line was busy, and the other time I got the machine. Forget it. You call me. I will give you back whatever the cost is.*
>
> *Love from Dad and Me*

And now for la pièce de résistance. I was looking for a long hooded fur jacket to keep me warm, because my lectures take me to some of the coldest parts of the country in the dead of

winter. I searched for a jacket, checking all the furriers in Hart-
ford and New Haven, but I couldn't afford anything they had. Finally, in desperation, I thought of the old family furrier. I called
my mother in Florida and said, "Mom, is Mr. Walowitz in Brook-
lyn still in business?" And she said, "Of course he's still in business. In fact his son is in the business with him, and his grandson
is twenty-three already, and he's in the business too. You call him
and I'm sure he'll make something for you in your price range."
When I told my Mom I had ordered a jacket from him, this is
what she wrote:

> Dear Doll,
> I think you are doing the right thing by going to Walowitz. I have
> always been very happy with everything he ever did for me. But tell
> him he should give you the cost of your trips to Brooklyn, and also
> don't pay taxes. TELL HIM I SAID SO. Explain to Walowitz that it
> costs you $25 each time you come to Brooklyn, and also tell him you
> are not going to charge him for the time it takes you. I am not joking.
> He should do something for you. Remind him that he didn't give you
> a wedding gift!
>
> Love from Dad and Me

Recently, at the conclusion of my lectures on the importance
of humor, a nice Chinese man came over to me and said, "Joyce,
I want you to know that having heard your mother's letters, I
now know there is a universality in mothers. I also realize my
mother must be Jewish!"

JOYCE M. SALTMAN

LUCY, ETHEL, AND ME

om, listen!" eight-year-old Meredith exclaimed, pulling on my arm, giggling. "Lucy and Ethel are working in a chocolate factory to make some money. It's easy at first, but then the chocolate keeps coming faster and faster and faster." She stopped to take a breath. "So they're eating it, and they've stuffed their mouths *full*. And it still keeps coming. Mom!"

"I'm listening." I sighed. "But I'm trying to get ready for my presentation."

"Can I help?"

"Not tonight. I'm in a hurry." I motioned to the two black suitcases and the stacks of sample clothing—embroidered polos and corporate casual shirts— freshly ironed and folded.

"I wish you had your old job." Meredith was dressed in a nightgown, her long brown hair pulled up in a ponytail. Freckles splashed across her upturned nose as she leaned closer, dark eyes opened wide, waiting for my comment. When I made none, she stomped away to watch the old shows on *Nick at Nite*. I packed my samples and set my alarm clock, dreading the three-hour drive to my nine A.M. appointment.

My contact for the meeting had visited our facility. Together we had watched blank T-shirts rotate from station to station on the automatic textile printer while squeegees pushed a myriad of thick colored inks across the screens, making elaborate designs. Nimble-fingered seamstresses pushed cloth-cap panels beneath bobbing needles. Printers with ink-stained hands stacked sheets of paper into Heidelberg presses that cranked out newsletters that day. Wouldn't everyone like the convenience of one-stop shopping for screen printing, cap manufacturing, embroidery, and award-winning offset printing and artwork?

I thought so when I had joined the fast-growing company two years earlier. I told friends, "I have found my niche. I will write and be creative." I soon learned the company suffered from serious growing pains. My vision of producing four-color brochures and ad campaigns dissipated into selling marketing services, managing sales reps, handling production problems, and preparing last-minute sales reports for bankers. We secured national projects, but it wasn't enough. The company was sold. Now I crammed information from catalogues and price lists because there was no time to learn the intricacies that came with the day-in, day-out selling of apparel.

"You look exhausted," the receptionist said the morning after my presentation when I asked about my calls. I tried to smile. "I got the account," I said, then I dashed to my office. Inside, mounds of paperwork waited. Meredith's second-grade school picture stood on my desk. Her smile tugged at me. I missed being with her as I had been before. Had we spent enough time together lately?

I didn't have time to wonder. Employees stormed my office with paychecks in hand. One after another said, "Have you seen this?" A memo from the management attached to the paycheck said, "All employees have been assigned a number. Each employee must punch a time clock. We are presently reviewing employee health benefits."

As senior vice president, I tried to reassure them: "The new owner has the working capital to keep the business going." Inwardly, I worried. Did his plan include me?

Over the next few weeks, my assistant resigned and others found termination letters on their desks. Morale plummeted, tempers flared, and even old-timers grumbled, "It's not fun anymore." More and more accounts demanded my attention. But was it bad enough to give up my salary? With all phone lines ringing, I felt trapped in Lucy and Ethel's chocolate-factory nightmare.

Several weeks later, I returned home from a late meeting. I tiptoed into Meredith's bedroom and watched her sleep. The clock ticked. Had she grown while I was away? Nearby, my early morning note to her said, "Have fun at school. Mom loves you." After a while, I kissed her forehead.

"Mama," she said, opening her sleepy eyes, "is making a living the same as making a life?" *Out of the mouths of babes.*

The answer was easy. "No," I said, knowing the letter I would type after she was fast asleep would begin, "It is with regret that I submit my resignation. . . ."

DEBRA AYERS BROWN

> *"A child is fed with milk and praise."*
> —MARY LAMB

THE I AM'S

*I*t's not easy disciplining your children. It's one of the hardest jobs handed to any new mom or dad. Many parents today were brought up with spankings, a method our parents used to teach us right from wrong.

When my first child was nine months old, he was able to pull himself up from the floor to the coffee table and stand on his own. I thought this was absolutely wonderful. I knew it wouldn't be too long before he would be learning to walk.

But when he turned two, I found he would pull things off of the coffee table. I would smack his little fingers and say, "No, don't touch." By the time he turned four, smacking his little fingers was no longer working. I tried telling him, "Be good," but it didn't work. No matter how many times I'd repeat myself, he never seemed to listen. I sounded like a broken record: "Be still," "Don't play with the VCR," "Sit down!" "Don't misbehave at day care," and "Don't run in the street!"

In desperation, I decided to talk with my father, who, with my mother, had raised ten children. How did they do it? How did they make all of us behave? When I told my father about my son's behavior problems, he suggested, "Why not sit him down and talk to him?" This was a surprise to me because he had raised us up on spankings. I couldn't help but think that, over the years, Dad must have discovered that spankings weren't always the answer. I decided to take Dad's advice, but what should I say, and how could I change my son's way of thinking? I realized that if I could change how he thought of himself, he could change his behavior.

The next time I found myself frustrated and exhausted with my son's antics, I sat him down in his little chair, and I said, "Son, repeat after me."

I am smart
I am talented
I am creative
I am trustworthy
I am loyal
I am truthful
I am athletic
I am loving
I am kind
I am brilliant
I am skillful
I am honest, and most of all
I am beautiful

I'm really not sure what inspired me at that moment to come up with and begin saying the I Am's. But the first time I tried it, I remember looking at my son's dear face and listening to him repeat the I Am's back to me in earnest. It made me flash back to when I used to imagine having children and wanting nothing but success for them. I saw a child that could grow up to be sensational instead of someone I didn't know. In the beginning, he may not have fully understood each word, but I could tell he understood the intent.

My son had occasion to repeat the I Am's a number of times

during his early years, and he grew to understand the meaning of each one. He's now in the fourth grade and is a straight-A student. He is a part of an after-school writing club, sings in the school choir, plays the trumpet, takes piano lessons, has taught himself to swim, and he plans to enroll in the summer league for bowling. Most of all, my son doesn't get spankings anymore.

I believe in the I Am's, and I continue to add to them often. I now use the I Am's with my two daughters as well. By incorporating the I Am's into their way of thinking, my children have learned to believe in themselves with each positive action they take.

JOY BOYD

THE WISDOM OF THE RUG

*T*he sound of an early-morning alarm clock signals get-up-and-go or grumbling, depending on one's inner clock. As a morning lover, I perk with the coffee at 5:00 A.M. My former college roommate—one of those thrive-after-five (P.M.) types—often reminds me how irritating morning exuberance is to those who would like to skip mornings altogether.

Perhaps my love of mornings centers on a habit formed over the years. Each morning, I gravitate to my favorite quiet place, my rug. My children can attest to the care that goes into selecting the *perfect* rug, since at 5:00 A.M., it becomes my altar of spiritual inspiration, hope, prayer, and grace.

The discipline of "rug sitting" began during uncertain days in the cancer recovery process, when fear swirled like a tornado around my heart. The rug was a haven where tears flowed with abandon. The process of pouring thoughts into journal pages while sitting on the rug helped me to focus on priorities and rearrange my future goals. Reading, writing, and listening to the Voice of Guidance led to a renewed spiritual balance.

Peace was the natural byproduct from my time on the rug. Journeying through difficult days to an oasis of calm intensified my appreciation of the simple, ordinary pleasures in life, long taken for granted before the crisis event. My health is now fully restored, but the rug remains a place of praise, pondering, and play.

Rug time allows the creativity in my work to flow freely. And rug time also allows me to be grateful—for those who have passed yet left an indelible ink print on my life, for those in the present who continue to bless my life, and for those who will decorate my future.

Several months ago, our son Chad called while traveling abroad. He said he had purchased a "memory gift" for himself. My curiosity was really piqued. When he came home with his treasure, he couldn't wait to show me. Not realizing how my rug ritual had inadvertently rubbed off on my son, I was surprised when Chad unwrapped a magnificent handwoven Moroccan carpet.

He has entrusted it to our care until it takes a special place in his home—where like mother, like son, he'll one day weave upon his own rug an even richer life.

CANDIS FANCHER

GOODBYE, EDDIE

He came out of the woods, and he must have known I was completely vulnerable. I had vowed there would never be another, but there he was, tempting me, making me feel wanted.

I don't know how I knew it, but his name just sprang from my lips. "Eddie. You're Eddie, aren't you?" I think he nodded, but sometimes it's hard to tell with cats. Anyway, he seemed to want the warm leftover breakfast oatmeal with milk and sugar. He seemed to like the buttered toast. He didn't turn down the bacon either. As a matter of fact, I never saw a cat eat that much in one sitting.

Eddie was scraggly, with that kind of devil-may-care, James Dean look. He was a guy you wanted to trust, but you knew down deep that you shouldn't. I thought all these thoughts as I reached out to pet Eddie and he turned his head up to me so that I could scratch his neck.

My beloved Kimi, a cat that lived in our house for thirteen years, had recently died. I vowed no more cats! No more attachments to animals. No more maternal responsibility to nonhumans. Then Eddie walked into my life, from out of the woods.

Eddie was a gray tomcat. He had only half his tail, and he didn't seem to mind the barrage of jokes that were directed at his very obvious defect. Rather, he seemed to flaunt his half-tail, as if somehow it was a better tail simply because it was different from most.

Whereas my Kimi ate only dry cat food from the bag, I noticed my maternal instincts moving into high gear when I found myself buying Eddie the very best canned cat food—he seemed to need it more. Whereas Kimi would jump on my lap and sit and purr as long as I would permit, Eddie directed his life on his own terms. He would much prefer to stretch out on the cool tile floor than sit on my lap. And he seemed to get along with many other animals. Kimi never could get used to dogs, but Eddie seemed to like them. Also, while Kimi used her private entrance to come and go as she pleased, Eddie preferred the back door. He preferred being let in and let out. He preferred having people do things for him.

Eddie stayed with me for a year and a half. During that time, I confided in him, but he remained the strong and silent type, the kind of guy you always wonder about. The kind who never reveals his thoughts.

Without a word, without a note, without a sign, Eddie left. I shouldn't have been surprised. I should have known that one day it would end. Maybe he was just too proud to be someone's cat. Maybe he found someone as vulnerable as I was that day he entered my life. Maybe he just got lost, like so many guys with that James Dean grin.

I'll always remember the delightful incongruity that was Eddie. He was all tomcat, but the only collar he'd wear happened to be delicate pink.

MARLENE R. JANNUSCH

LEAVING HOME:
A MOTHER'S PERSPECTIVE

I blinked back tears as I gazed out the car window at a smirking orange moon. To me, at least, it seemed to be smirking, but maybe that was just my state of mind. Our car sped east into the darkness, and with each revolution of the wheels, it took me farther away from my daughter, my eldest child.

Several hours earlier, my husband and I had left her in a dormitory at Middle Tennessee State University, a twelve-hour drive from our home in Manassas, Virginia.

I had been so proud of myself as I'd said goodbye to Leah. Earlier, she'd pleaded with me not to cry—not until after we'd left her, anyway, and I hadn't. But I'd come close. As we rode down in the dormitory elevator together, Leah had been silent, keeping her eyes carefully averted from my face. I, however, couldn't stop gazing at her, trying, I guess, to imprint these last moments with her on my brain. I wouldn't be seeing her again until Christmas. My eyes lingered on a tiny scar on her forehead, an upside-down "v."

A memory flashed in my mind of a fifteen-month-old Leah pulling a clock-radio off a bedside table right in front of me. It seemed to happen in slow motion. I saw the radio falling toward her and tried to catch it, but I couldn't move fast enough. The next thing I knew, Leah was screaming, her forehead dripping blood. At the emergency room, I wept in my husband's arms, listening to my toddler shrieking, "Mommy . . . Mommy . . .

Mommy" in the cubicle next door as the cut was stitched up. Her panicked cries broke my heart, and I wished I could trade places with her. Suffer the pain for her so she wouldn't have to.

There have been many, many other times since that day that I've had the same wish—her first day in a new school when she tried so bravely to hide her anxiety, the time she didn't have a date for the homecoming dance but all her friends did, and the bleak January day in her junior year when a classmate was killed in a car accident. All those times, I wanted to take away her pain, but I knew I couldn't do it.

Just as she couldn't take away my pain as our car sped down the interstate while the miles between us lengthened and the orange moon smirked down on me in my aching sadness. But I knew my pain was only temporary. As the days passed, I would adjust to a different life without my daughter in the house.

With that adjustment in mind, I decided to redecorate Leah's room, keeping her bed and dresser but converting a section into a sewing area for me. A few weeks after we left her at college, I began to pack up the few items she'd left behind. I felt quite strong as I sifted through yearbooks, photo albums, and various odds and ends she'd collected throughout the years. But suddenly, I came across an item that shattered my emotional calm.

I picked up a green square of burlap imprinted with two small handprints in white. My eyes blurred as I read the typewritten message above the handprints, and I could no longer hold back my tears.

Sometimes you get discouraged
Because I am so small
And always leave my fingerprints
On furniture and walls.
But every day I am growing
And soon I'll be so tall,
That all those little handprints

Will be hard to recall.
So here's a final handprint
To remember, Mother dear
Exactly how my fingers looked
In Sunday School this year.
                1980

I cried unashamedly—and it felt good.

CAROLE BELLACERA

III

THE INTUITIVE EDGE

"There are two worlds: the world that we can
measure with line and rule,
and the world that we feel
with our hearts and imagination."

—LEIGH HUNT

A MOTHER'S INTUITION

One day I sat on our backyard deck with two-week-old Philip cradled against my chest. Philip's two-year-old brother, Christopher, played beside me. My husband tinkered below, fixing the lawn mower.

I asked my husband to watch Christopher while I went inside. Christopher happily toddled down the stairs to his father, play mower in hand. As I watched him go down each step, satisfied that he and Dad were together, I brought Philip inside to the changing table.

As I began to diaper Philip, I suddenly felt a surge of dread and a compelling sensation that was pulling me back outside. I ran to the deck leaving Philip unstrapped and naked on the changing table—a practice I've never before or since risked.

The steep roof on our garage hangs partially over the deck. With a chair, a child can easily climb onto the roof, which is exactly what Christopher had done. By now, he was straddling the peak, one foot on each side.

I looked up just as he lifted his left foot into the air. In a split second he'd be stepping over the roof's edge and plummeting to the concrete driveway below. I let out a sound that can only be described as a wail, a bellow of pure terror.

Christopher froze. My husband ran toward us. I flew onto the roof as if I had wings, leaving my body behind. Calmly, I pulled Christopher's small body toward me and simply sat there on the roof's apex, holding him in my arms.

Only after I retrieved Philip from the nursery, and only after the four of us sat safely planted in our deck chairs, did I begin to shake.

I do not know what pulled me outside that day. I understand how adrenaline could enable me to scale the roof so rapidly, yet I cannot say what yanked me initially and insistently outside, like the tugging of an invisible lasso.

I am not a mother who takes chances. I would not have left any newborn unattended on a high table. Yet I opened to a subtle and pervasive intuitive force that exists in all mothers—just in time to save my child's life.

ANNE SPOLLEN

PALE-BLUE LETTERS

*B*abysitting my friend's son is always an experience. Jeb has been diagnosed with some autistic characteristics, but it's not his disorder that gets to me—it's the way other people react to him that can ruin my day.

Jeb is different. He isn't interested in demonstrations of affection and rarely looks anyone in the eye. If you speak too loudly, he'll cover his ears and scream at the top of his lungs. Touch him and he'll cry out as if in great pain.

We walk to the park every day, but not to play with other children; he doesn't enjoy making friends. He only likes hanging out on one particular swing. He'll sway for hours, rocking back and forth. Even though he has an expensive play center of his own in his backyard, it's only on this one swing in the middle of the local playground that he'll play.

Since I've been babysitting him for years, I know what he enjoys, and I allow him almost everything that he wants: the walk to the park, the swing, and his favorite box of crayons when we get home in the evenings. Drawing and writing are usually how he spends most of his nights. He invariably chooses a worn, pale-blue crayon. Then I tuck him into bed and read to him from one of my poetry collections until he falls asleep.

Jeb has never told me he loves me, but rarely does he get into trouble. If he starts to get agitated in public, all I have to do is hand him something to write with; he'll instinctively sit down and stay busy, penning nonsensical words and doodles.

Today at the park I had a mother pull her own child away

from Jeb so the child wouldn't "catch" what Jeb has. Another father inquired, "What's wrong with him?" As always, I avoided responding.

When I brought Jeb home, I found his mother reduced to tears. She is often like this. The stress of raising a child who never shows affection tends to wear on a mother after a while.

I sat down at the kitchen table beside her. "What's the matter, Shara?"

Sniffling, she wept. "I gave some of Jeb's papers to an autistic specialist to try and figure out what's going on in his mind, what he's trying to say."

I patted her hand, thinking those scribbles and pictures weren't anything anyone could understand.

"Dr. Matovski told me the pictures were exceptional and increasingly intricate. He said Jeb's words are poetry! The letters and sentences are just backwards!"

"Really?" I gasped. "You mean the stuff Jeb writes actually makes sense!"

She gulped in ragged breaths, pulling out one of Jeb's pieces of construction paper from her purse. "Look."

I glanced down over Jeb's pale-blue crayon scribbles and noticed there were words underneath where the doctor, a pediatric neurologist, must have transcribed.

> *In the darkness I do lie*
> *Liking the quiet and the night*
> *As she reads a poem of a guy*
> *Who's not afraid of doing what's right.*

> *In my heart I yearn to be*
> *As strong as the hero's will*
> *Whose spirit was unfettered and free*
> *But whose love for women was grander still.*

Yet my love hides within my soul
Afraid to break the chains.
But withholding my emotions has taken its toll
And for my caretakers only heartache remains.

So to these two women I write this poem
To let them know how happy I am.
Their love is greater than anything I've known
And it's helping me to become a man.

—Jeb

Together, we collapsed into tears, barely able to comprehend that all this time, Jeb has been feeling fulfilled and appreciating us, loving us.

We were still embracing one another and crying when the phone rang.

"Hello," my friend answered.

"Hello, Shara. This is Dr. Matovski. I just finished transcribing the rest of Jeb's poetry. He surely has some savant abilities. Some of these are quite fascinating. Would you mind if I showed them to a friend of mine, Frank Paterno?"

"Frank Paterno?"

I heard the name and knew he owned a local publishing house.

"Sure," Shara answered. "But first send me more information explaining how you deciphered Jeb's poetry. I want to be able to read them for myself now."

"Of course, Shara. I hope you're very proud of your son. He's a very well-adjusted, talented young boy," Dr. Matovski told her.

It's been over a year since that night, and Jeb has now had two poems published in a book made to help raise funds for handicapped children. I'm not sure which his mother is more proud of, his being a poet or just being a "happy" little boy.

I believe it's the latter.

And for me, well, I remain their babysitter. We still have our daily routine of walking to the park, playing on the swing set, writing, drawing, and reading poetry at night. But now when a mother or father asks me what's wrong with him, I remember the pale-blue letters and say, "Nothing. He's perfect."

MICHELE WALLACE-CAMPANELLI

If you have enough fantasies, you're ready
in the event that something happens.
—SHEILA BALLANTYNE

THE FORTUNETELLER

My husband and I took a short trip to New Orleans several years ago for some much-needed time to ourselves, away from our two little boys, ages seven and five. We wanted to think about the next chapter in our lives. We had enjoyed our children so much as babies, preschoolers, and now, "big boys." Soon they would both be in school, and I was thinking of returning to the world of journalism. We could certainly use another paycheck. And yet the sight of babies curled against their mothers left me with a deep maternal longing.

My husband and I checked into a hotel in the French Quarter and spent the next three days wandering through antique stores, galleries, bookstores, places that did not lend themselves to noisy little boys. We ate exotic food in quiet, candlelit restaurants and stayed out late listening to jazz. We took an eerie tour of the local graveyard and heard stories about voodoo and ghosts.

New Orleans worked its magic on me, and I found myself in a shop that sold crystal balls and special tea leaves. A sign behind the counter said that someone could see my future, if I cared to pay. What the heck. I made an appointment.

"Nancy" was a woman with long brown hair who wore a loose cotton dress that reached to the floor. She pulled aside the beads that hung in a small doorway and invited me into a room that smelled of incense. She carefully spread out Tarot cards and began to talk with me about my life. Hmmmm. She saw that I was good at the work I did. That more work was around the corner. That I would be successful. And then she stopped looking at the cards and looked into my eyes.

"Are you thinking of having more children?" she asked.

My eyes filled with water, and I felt my stomach turn over. "Of course not" was what I meant to say.

"Yes," I answered.

She'd hit a nerve, and she was pleased. "Nancy" told me that the child was wanting to be born (more tears from me) and that I could expect a girl. A girl! I thought the fortuneteller had looked straight into my heart.

My husband and I were in agreement that we weren't finished with the sleepless days of diapers, *Sesame Street*, and toys spread across the floor. The romantic setting of New Orleans was a catalyst for our decision. We returned home with a new plan for the future.

When I told my sister about my visit to the fortuneteller, she howled with laughter. "How could you have fallen for that one?" she teased.

But several weeks later, she found herself in New Orleans on a business trip with her husband. She called one night, obviously taken with the spirit of the French Quarter, and asked for directions to the fortune-teller's shop. The next day she was sitting in front of a woman with long brown hair. After some discussion, the woman said she could see that my sister was good at her profession. That more work and great success were around the corner. Then she stopped and looked at my sister. She said, "Are you thinking of having more children?"

My sister hooted at that. Absolutely not! Her kids were adolescents, and she was done with babies. Oh. The fortuneteller went on to other things, including a big move her family would make very soon. (The big move never materialized.)

Now six years later, I smile at this memory as I listen to my third son playing with trucks and blocks in the next room, alongside his two older brothers. I remember my reaction to the fortuneteller's vision, and I think: So many times, when we think we're listening to what the other person is saying, we're really listening to ourselves.

TONI WOOD

STORIES OF THE RED LAMP

Most children dread bedtime; at my grandmother's house, I cherished it. Grandma, a giant bear of a woman, would squat down beside me, take my hands in hers, and tickle the back of my skull with her intense blue-eyed gaze. "Are you and your brothers ready for bed?" she'd ask.

I would nod and run to gather my two younger brothers, then set up the three cots we slept on, nestled close together, in her living room. We spread sleeping bags over the nylon and metal beds, then climbed into the warmth, ready and waiting for Grandma to come in and tell us a bedtime story.

After a few minutes she would amble in and take her place on the scarlet couch. The intense color of the couch matched the rest of the decor well. On the floor lay an enormous red oriental rug stretching the entire length of the room. The window, framed by heavy red velvet drapes and white transparent linens, did not seem to overlook a suburban street in Minnesota, but instead opened onto a world limited only by our imaginations. In this ornate room that mimicked a Victorian boudoir, filled with the treasures of a lifetime of garage sales, the most wonderful of all the objects were the matching antique red glass lamps.

"Are you ready?" Grandma would ask, ceremoniously turning

the curled iron keys to illuminate each red glass lamp. "Do you see the path of light coming from the lamps?" Grandma would question as we snuggled farther down into our sleeping bags and squinted our eyes.

"Yes, we can see it!" the three of us replied on cue and in unison.

"Now, do you see those three little children walking on that path into the red lamp? Do you see them?"

"Yes, Grandma! Yes!"

Grandma then launched into a story of the three children— a girl and her two younger brothers—and their adventures in Red Lamp Land. Only magic, love, and peace existed in Red Lamp Land; the outside world never imposed here. We left our parents' messy divorce behind at the base of the lighted red path. In Red Lamp Land, Grandma's words soothed our fears. We three children conquered all foes, maneuvered skillfully through danger, and aspired to great heights. In Red Lamp Land, my brothers and I, working together, were invincible.

The stories about the red lamps ended a long time ago. The last time I saw Grandma, a few months ago, Alzheimer's had overwhelmed her mind and she seemed to have taken up permanent residence in the land of her own imagination. Yet I believe her to be happy; I know the world in her mind to be a rich and satisfying place. I sought shelter there myself during the most difficult days of my childhood.

In the twilight of her life, I will take her hand in mine as she readies for her long slumber. I smile as I think of her watching for the path of light that will lead her to the special place where only magic, love, and peace exist, where the outside world never intrudes. She should know the route well. She has traveled it in her dreams many times. And the children she taught to stick together, to face adversity in unison, will courageously surround

her as the light dims on this world, and illuminates for her a
heavenly place.

JACQUELYN B. FLETCHER

SHE'S JUST LIKE YOU

*he sun warmed my back as I stood on a snow-covered peak overlooking Squaw Valley and the deep turquoise waters of Lake Tahoe.

David's affectionate nudge in the ribs halted my meditations. "I know what that means," I replied, brushing wind teased hair from my face. "You always poke me like that when you're thinking and you want to share it with me."

"I am and I do," he said, smiling down at me. "When you get your daughter, you've got to bring her up here. I'll teach her to ski." Then he laughed and said, "Of course, since I'm also the big city boy, I'll tour the galleries with her, show her how to dress, and acquaint her little palate with only the finest cuisine. And I'd better familiarize her with the kitchen, because your cooking is utterly ordinary."

"Hey, watch it!" I said. I searched my friend's handsome face for the real purpose behind our conversation and reminded him, "Did you forget I've been disqualified to adopt a child ten times now? Even if it happens within the next few years, I'm close to fifty. Do you actually believe it will ever happen?"

"Of course I do. Look out there," he said waving a gloved hand toward the fresh pack of snow and the beautifully wooded sections of high bluffs. "That's a universal miracle—and you're a part of the universe. So, Donna, believe a child is in your future."

I cast a lopsided grin at David, wishing I possessed his natural charm and confidence and that like him, I could afford only the finest ski attire. "You are so positive, David. I gain such strength from you. And would you believe I'm the motivational speaker?"

I didn't know then, standing atop that mountain, it would be the last time we would ski together. David had a great fighting spirit, but a short while later, the HIV virus would allow disease to ravage his body. He was barely forty years old when he lost his battle with AIDS and passed on.

I never really came to terms with his death until a year later, when I visited his grave. With tears pooling in my eyes, I found myself talking to him as though we were still together on that mountain. I said, "You won't believe it, David, the most wonderful thing has happened. I've been matched up with a birth mother and father. They're going to have a baby daughter and they want me to be the mom."

In that instant, I clearly heard David's voice, as if he were standing beside me. "I know," he said, "in fact she's here with me right now. I'm telling her all about you: Your off-the-wall stubbornness, driving energy, your madcap humor, how you love sports and love to have a good time." Then I heard that contagious laugh of his. "I know patience is not your strong point, Donna, so I'll tell you now—she'll be born on June twentieth. On that date, her spirit will join her body. And Donna, she'll be just like you. She'll have your energy, your coloring, and your eyes and you two will have a laughing good time together."

I knew I had "heard" the truth from David, yet a few weeks later when I learned the date of the birth mother's scheduled cesarean delivery, June 23, I began experiencing doubt. Had I merely imagined David's graveside message?

I had almost put it out of my mind until the evening of June 20, when I answered the phone. A woman on the other end said, "Your birth mother asked me to make this call. She went into early labor and your beautiful nine-pound four-ounce baby daughter was born today at 6:06 P.M." Overjoyed, I could hardly speak. I mumbled my thanks and told her I would arrive on the first plane in the morning. David's words danced through my mind. From the bottom of my heart, I realized no matter where you find it, truth is truth.

Today, when I take my daughter to the park, or we're out together, my friends shake their heads and say, "Donna, her mannerisms and looks are incredibly you." I just smile and say, "I know. I was told she'd be just like me."

DONNA HARTLEY

"All success begins with a quality decision to the vision."
—ANONYMOUS

LOST AND FOUND

I landed at the Los Angeles International Airport at 9:20 P.M. recently after flying back from Hawaii. My feet hurt and were swollen, and I was bone-tired. I'd been having a day of mishaps, so I wasn't surprised to find chaos in baggage claim as we all tripped over one another, struggling to find our bags and get out of the airport.

Miraculously, in under an hour I'd retrieved my luggage, hailed a cab, and was home. After unpacking, I collapsed into a hot bath. It felt like heaven as I submerged myself right up to the bottom of my lower lip. I shut my eyes, drew a long breath, and let my mind drift as I let go of the day.

All of a sudden, a jolt of adrenaline hit me hard, and I bolted upright. I couldn't remember bringing my canvas carry-on into the house. I leapt out of the tub and threw a towel around myself. I tore through our house, dripping wet, looking for my little white canvas bag with the pretty blue dolphins on the side. I had bought it in Hawaii and used it as an extra carry-on. In it was a newspaper, a couple of magazines, a bottle of Champagne . . . and my jewelry! I had put my jewelry bag in it with all my priceless pieces. My diamond earrings, my diamond necklace, anniversary and birthday gifts from my husband. My black pearls that I'd gotten in Tahiti. Beautiful things, but their sentimental value was what I prized above all. Gone!

By now, it was 11:30 P.M. I frantically called the airport and got one of those infuriating recordings with a menu that led me in circles, so I hung up.

Memories streamed in of the special moments when my husband had given me these gifts, and I choked back tears. I closed my eyes and prayed to God for help. An answer came like quicksilver.

I had a vision that appeared in three distinct parts. First, I saw an angelic-looking being. A small, very old man, luminescent, with an extremely long white beard that came to a point near his waist. He was floating about six inches off the ground guarding my canvas bag. His angelic presence was so majestic that my little bag with the blue dolphins looked undeserving, even silly, sitting at his feet. Then, I saw a man's hand giving me my bag just as I had left it. Finally, I saw a clock that read 12:48. Immediately a profound feeling of peace and calm swept over me, and I knew everything was going to be okay.

The vision and warm feeling stayed with me as I drove back to the airport. I pulled up in front of baggage claim. It was oddly deserted. I looked for parking but saw only a taxi zone. I thought of how tough the parking enforcement is at LAX, but no one was around, so I took a chance and parked in front anyway.

I ran to the door and gave it a good yank. It was locked! My calm started to evaporate. I pressed my forehead against the window, searching the empty cavernous room to see if the bag was where I left it. I couldn't tell. I banged on the glass door, but there wasn't a soul around. Tears welled up. How could my vision and the calm feeling I had be so wrong?

After several minutes, an older man in a security guard uniform entered the baggage claim area. I pounded on the door again and got his attention. He ambled over and unlocked the door. I tried not to sound too panicked. "Hi. I came in on a

United flight tonight, and I left my carry-on bag by the carousel. Can I come in and look for it?"

"Oh, I'm sorry, but this area is closed," he answered. "No more baggage comin' in here tonight."

"But sir, I'll be just one minute," I pleaded. "I left it right over there." I pointed. I searched his eyes and knew he could see I was frantic. He let me in.

I ran to the spot where I had left it, but it wasn't there! My level of anxiety was increasing. "Sir, sir, could you please check in your lost and found? It's a small white canvas bag with blue dolphins on the side."

"I'm sorry, ma'am, but lost and found is closed," he replied. "I don't have a key to get in there. But I wouldn't worry about it. They'll call you tomorrow if your phone number is on your I.D. tag, or you can call—"

I quickly cut him off, "No, no, you don't understand. I have no I.D. tag on the bag. My name is not on it anywhere!"

"Oh, I see. . . ." His voice trailed off. I could tell he thought my bag was gone.

"Could you please just look in the back . . . somewhere . . . anywhere?" I said in a desperate tone.

"If it's here," he explained, "it's not gonna be anywhere except lost and found, ma'am." He broke off and sighed, knowing I wasn't going away until he looked. "What does it look like again?" he asked wearily. I described my bag, and he wandered off behind an unmarked door.

I was feeling hopeful again until my peripheral vision caught a glimpse of red lights blinking outside. I turned to see a parking enforcement officer get out of his car and walk around mine, ticket pad in hand.

I ran to the door and yelled to him, "Officer, please don't give me a ticket! I lost my carry-on bag, and a gentleman is in the back looking for it. Please, just give me two minutes. Please!" The heavyset, stone-faced officer glanced at me with complete disregard. Then, as if something changed his mind, he turned and gave me a look that appeared to be one of consideration. He checked his watch. "You've got two minutes," he stated firmly.

"Thank you!" I sang out, and I raced back inside. I scanned the area for the security guard, and came to a dead halt in the middle of baggage claim, staring at an endless stream of unmarked doors along the perimeter.

This is impossible, I thought. Nothing was going the way I thought it would. Then, out of one of those doors, came the guard—carrying my little white canvas bag! He strolled toward me as if in slow motion. The blue dolphins appeared as though they were jumping over waves as the bag swung back and forth under his grip. My heart was pounding. I looked at his hand, and just as it was in my vision, he held my bag up to me!

"Is this it?" he asked casually.

"Yes, yes it is," I squealed. I looked inside. Everything was just as I had left it. "I . . . I can't . . . thank you enough!" I said, my voice choked with emotion.

He shook his head, perplexed. "Can't imagine what it was doing back there. Shoulda been in lost and found." Still shaking his head as he sauntered away, he muttered again, "Shoulda been in lost and found."

I half-ran, half-skipped back to the car, where the officer was still hovering. "Here I come!" I hollered joyfully.

He saw me coming and laughed. "This must be your lucky day!" He smiled brightly and put his pad away.

"You have no idea how lucky, officer," I rejoiced. "Thank you!"

While driving home, I chuckled to myself as I thought about the events of the past couple of hours. How clearly I'd seen my vision, and then how easily doubts took over when things didn't look as though they were going my way.

When I pulled into our dark garage, I just sat in the car feeling totally humble and extremely grateful for the divine assistance sent my way. As I let it all sink in, I realized this was not about

material possessions. My incredible vision was a gift. My lesson
was trusting in the power of prayer, and surrendering to how it
operates in my life.

Before I pulled the keys out of the ignition, my eyes were
drawn to the clock illuminated on the dashboard. The time read
12:48.

TANNIS BENEDICT

ONE MORE CHANCE

*O*ne May evening in 1986, my husband had slipped quietly out of bed. Moments later I smelled his cigarette and heard him sobbing in the living room. I lay there in the darkness, knowing that something was terribly wrong. He had been distant for weeks now, or had it been months?

For a moment my mind drifted to a day the previous summer, to a time when it was me crying. A new stylist had butchered my hair, and I felt my precarious hold on beauty slipping away. My husband was unsympathetic. "Don't be ridiculous!" he had snapped in response to my tears. "It's just a haircut!"

That night, I felt his tears were about something much more serious. My heart was pounding when I pulled on my robe and joined him in the living room.

"Please tell me what's wrong," I said, although I feared what he had to tell me would be almost more than I could bear. My fears were justified.

"I don't want to be married to you anymore," said the man who had told me so many times before that he would love me forever. The pain was so intense I could scarcely breathe. "My feelings for you have changed," he confessed. "I don't see a future for us together." *This can't be happening. I can't let him go! I'll do anything!*

"Please," I begged through almost uncontrollable sobs, "please give me one more chance." But his mind had been made up long before tonight, and nothing I said changed the fact that my four-year marriage was over.

The years passed, and so did my fear that I could never love again. Five years after my divorce, I stood in a church and exchanged vows with my second husband. We promised to stay together until "death do us part," but in the back of my mind, I remembered sharing those vows before and how shallow those words had proved to be.

One February evening several years into the marriage, the daily struggles and arguments over money had become almost unbearable, and I had given up hope that our life together would improve. For several weeks, I had been planning how to end my second marriage.

That night I found the courage and told my husband, "We have to talk." A feeling of heaviness spread across my chest. He said he'd sensed that something was wrong. We both began weeping. In between sobs, he told me how much he loved me, and that he wanted me to be happy. With my resolve still intact, he packed his things quickly so that he could leave.

But before he left, he turned to me with a heartbroken look and said, "Please give me one more chance." I thought, *No. It's too late. Nothing will change.* But my heart heard only a haunting echo of something I had once wanted so desperately for myself.

Until that point, I thought I was certain of my path. Then something inside me shifted, and suddenly I knew I must give my second marriage the opportunity my first marriage never had. The heavy feeling in my chest lifted.

The next few years were not easy. They were filled with false starts and and many challenges as we attempted to rekindle our marriage. But I learned that love is a choice. And there were even more moments of discovery, growth, and joy than I could have ever imagined as we created our love anew.

One evening, years after the night I wanted to end my second marriage, I was deep in thought and reflecting back on my change of heart. So deep in thought, I wasn't paying attention to the task at hand—trimming my hair. With a slip of the scissors, I had a set of what appeared to me to be hideously short and crooked bangs. I had an important presentation to give the next day, and despite my efforts at "personal growth" over the years, I still cared too much about how I looked.

While tears rolled down my cheeks, I went into the living room where my husband was sitting. "I'm not beautiful anymore," I cried. He looked up at me from his magazine, and for an instant I was transported back to a summer day more than a decade ago.

But this was a different time.

The man I almost pushed away gazed at me with a mixture of love and sympathy. He then got up, took me in his arms, and gently stroked my hair.

TAG GOULET

FAMILY CONNECTIONS

I *flew to San Francisco recently for a speaking ap-*
pearance, and my husband called me from home. Very excitedly, he relayed the events of the day.

After our daughter, Emily, left the house to see a movie with a
girlfriend, a young man in her class named Adam placed a ten-
foot homemade sign on our garage door that said, "Homecoming '97—Adam?" Then he lined the driveway and the sidewalk all
the way up to the front door with chocolate kisses. On the
doorstep he placed a red rose and a note that said, "Now that I
have 'kissed' the ground you walk on, will you go to the homecoming dance with me?"

Emily got on the phone, squealed with excitement, and filled
me in on the details. My first response to her: "Emily, I just have
one thing to say—marry him." Now, I know she is only fourteen
years old, but correct me if I'm wrong—she could do worse!

As I hung up the phone, my heart sank. I missed it! I *should*
have been there! What kind of parent am I? Guilt reared its ugly
head again. I flashed on the old TV series *Leave It to Beaver:* June
Cleaver, dressed to the nines at all times, bustling about in the
kitchen, always around when her children came home.

Left to myself in the quiet of the hotel room, I examined my
"shoulds" and asked myself, *But where is the problem?* Everyone
stayed "connected" in spite of my absence. Emily was floating
on air. Adam succeeded—the girl had said, "Yes!" Adam's mom,
who drove him to our house, sat in her car happily watching her
son make his rite of passage. (Why, not so long ago, she probably

couldn't get him to take a shower, and now he had transformed into Romeo asking Juliet for a date.) And my husband captured all the excitement on video. Magical moments punctuated my day in San Francisco as well. Hooking up with a dear friend for dinner capped a day of feeling very in tune with my audience, doing what I love to do.

I've discovered if we concentrate less on beating ourselves up over our self-imposed "should" list, and spend more time making quality connections with those we love, our lives will be richer.

When I viewed the situation from a "connection" point of view, I couldn't find a problem. Nothing to feel bad about.

The next week, Emily and I went out shopping for the perfect dress, matching shoes, and a slip that wouldn't show. When I told her how romantic and clever I thought Adam had been, she stopped in the middle of the mall, put her hands on her hips, looked at me warily, and said, "You're going to use this story in your talks, aren't you?"

I already had. We are so close, she knew what I'd do. I couldn't pass up a tale this good. My heart warmed, because she had me pegged. This daughter I so dearly love knows me so well that she can predict what I'll probably say or do. I realized I hadn't missed anything at all.

Like Paul Harvey wanting to relay "the rest of the story," let me tell you that they had a wonderful time at the dance, and for an evening, Emily looked like a twenty-year-old model. Unfortunately, she decided not to marry Adam. I've secretly kept his number in case she ever changes her mind!

MARY LoVERDE

IV
DIVINELY SENT

"There are two ways of spreading light: to be the candle
or the mirror that reflects it."

—EDITH WHARTON

THE VOICE OF GOD

*S*omehow *my grandparents, who were raising me, had* managed to survive the ravages of World War II in our native Hungary. But when that terrible war finally ended in 1945, no jubilation existed, because Soviet troops immediately held our country hostage in the arms of communism. All of a sudden, people who spoke out against these oppressions taking place were rounded up by the newly formed secret police force and never seen again.

My grandfather, a retired judge, continued to speak out freely, and in the fall of 1945, two men came to our house to get him. They said he was being taken in for questioning only. Grandfather, pointing out that his hands were dirty from working in the garden, asked if he could wash up first. The men agreed. When he didn't come out of the bathroom right away, they ran in and pushed the door open. The water in the sink was still running, but Grandfather had disappeared! He had jumped out the bathroom window and fled on foot.

After Grandfather went into hiding, life became even more difficult for Grandmother and me. We lived on soup made from the potatoes and other vegetables grown in our garden, and never knew when the secret police would show up to search our house again. Sometimes, they came in the middle of the night, breaking down the door in hopes of finding Grandfather. Fear became our constant companion, and prayer our sustenance.

For two years, my grandfather managed to elude capture, and although he sent word of his safety, most of the time we didn't know his whereabouts. Grandmother and I missed him terribly. The thought that we might never be together again plagued me constantly. But on a fall day in 1947, when I was ten years old, I knew exactly where to find him!

When new elections were held in our country, I waited for the results with great interest. The next morning our radio blared the news that the communist party had been defeated. Celebrations erupted in the streets, with none of us realizing that the communist government, backed by Soviet troops, wasn't about to give up, elections or no elections.

Certainly, after listening to the radio broadcast, my ten-year-old mind concluded the election results meant that Grandfather could come home and we could be a family again.

I wondered if Grandfather, who we recently heard was hiding out on a nearby farm, knew the good news. I decided now was the time to hike to the farm and tell him. Then we could come home together and surprise Grandmother! Of course, I didn't tell anyone of my plan. Rather than go to school, I set out on the long walk out of town to Grandfather's hiding place. As I reached the outskirts of our village without drawing attention to myself, wild anticipation filled my heart. In a short while I would see Grandfather for the first time in two years, and we would walk home together and live as a family again. My eyes filled with tears of joy with that thought, and I began to walk faster.

Startled, I suddenly heard a man's voice call my name. I stopped dead in my tracks and looked all around me, but saw no one. "Who are you? Where are you?" I asked, straining to see if he might be behind some nearby bushes.

"It isn't important where I am," the voice answered. "I'm here to warn you that you're putting your grandfather in grave danger, for you are being followed. Turn around and go back to your grandmother, immediately, and know that you will all be together again, soon."

Of course, I immediately turned and began running back toward the village, my heart pounding so hard I thought it would jump right out of my chest. I ran past a man on a bicycle and recognized him as one of the secret police. The voice had been right. I was being followed!

When I reached our house, I found Grandmother outside pacing back and forth in the street. "Oh, thank God you are all right! Someone came to tell me that you weren't in school and I thought they may have taken you," she said, gathering me in her arms.

"I decided to go and tell Grandfather that the communists lost the election," I wailed. Then I blurted out, "I thought we could come home together and surprise you!"

"Oh, my!" Grandmother shook her head.

"But a voice stopped me," I continued. "It told me I was being followed and to go back home. It was the kindest, most loving voice I ever heard, Grandmother. I believe it was the voice of God. No one else knew my plan."

My grandmother nodded, took me into the house, and held me for a long time. She told me everything would be better soon.

Two weeks later, a man came to get us in the middle of the night. By the time the sun rose, we had traveled to a place near the Austrian border where a large group of ethnic Germans were about to be deported into Austria. My heart sang when I saw Grandfather! He looked lovingly into my eyes and hugged me tightly. We were about to be smuggled out of Hungary as ethnic Germans. Recognizing the danger still around us, we didn't even breathe a sigh of relief until we crossed into Austria. There, we ended up in a refugee camp along with hundreds of other destitute refugees, but at least we were finally together.

Grandfather remained fearful that the long arm of communism could snatch him back. It wasn't until 1951, when we were given a chance at new lives in our wonderful new country, the United States of America, that he finally relaxed and lived out his life in grateful peace.

From time to time growing up, I'd wonder about the voice I heard that fall day in 1947. I'd even allow speculation when friends asked if the voice could have come from a neighbor who decided to warn me. But now, when I get very quiet and still, I know that voice, just as I recognized it as a child. Those loving, lifesaving words came from my God—the one who answers my prayers, clears my path, and lights my way.

RENIE SZILAK BURGHARDT

*"When circumstances seem to coincide in inexplicable ways,
the universe is reaching out to help you."*
—MARY MANIN MORRISSEY

THANKS, JOE

*B*ee-yer, getcha ice-cold beer,*"* echoed through Yankee Stadium. Peanuts, popcorn, and a zillion other smells wafted over the warm summer breeze as the crowd roared expectantly.

There was the man—long, lean Joltin' Joe DiMaggio—coming up to the plate; an unlikely hero for a demure little girl like me. Yet the Yankee Clipper went on to gain top spot in my personal Hall of Fame.

Years later, our fourteen-year-old son Larry made honor roll, became a hometown baseball star, and started avidly collecting baseball trivia. The sport ruled his life, and everyone just knew this kid would make it to the majors. No doubt about it.

We were a baseball family back then. Three or four evenings a week, plus weekends, we'd all rush through an early dinner and head out to the ballpark for games or practice.

Larry cheerfully took a job that summer that would help him reach another goal—buying himself a ten-speed bike. In spite of my concerns, he turned on his smiling charm and convinced me that our Connecticut hills required all those speeds. As usual with this lovable kid, I caved. He seemed so strong—so indestructible.

One afternoon, Larry took off on his beloved new bike for a quick swim before going to work. He never took that swim. He never arrived at work.

Coming down a hilly, curvy road, Larry and the bike hit a pile of sand. The bike stopped. Larry didn't. He sailed through the air, plummeted down a ravine, and hit a tree trunk—with his face.

Larry broke every blessed bone in his skull, as well as most bones in his face. Helmets for cyclists were unheard of back then.

A month or so later, after several surgeries, including a craniotomy, my boy came home. He walked into the house—a tall, bald, and disfigured skeleton—went into his room, and shut the door.

Our family's collective heart broke as the days and weeks went by. Other than visits to various doctors, Larry never ventured out. He didn't allow his friends in. It seemed as though his spirit had died.

The neurosurgeon told Larry, "No more contact sports, son, other than baseball, that is." Horrified that he would encourage my son to more risk, I questioned his reasoning. The doctor wisely explained, "While playing ball might be dangerous for Larry, to take away that part of his life could be worse."

As the months passed, I found myself wanting him to play ball, as box by box and folder by folder, Larry's baseball treasures came out of his room. "Throw these away," he'd mumble through wired jaws, "I don't want them anymore."

Late one afternoon, a close neighbor came by to see our reclusive son. As the father of his best friend, Russ passed muster with Larry and was allowed into his increasingly private sanctuary. A short while later, Larry came bounding down the hall. "Mom! Dad!" he called excitedly. "Look at this, will ya?" He held up a large autographed photograph of Joe DiMaggio. "I'm gonna show this to Jimmy and Mike." With that, he dashed out of the house and ran over the hill to find his buddies—for the first time in months.

Bewildered and amazed at the sudden turn of events, I couldn't wait to hear what had happened. We sat down as Russ, a private jet pilot for a business magnate, explained his latest flight. His only passenger that day had turned out to be Joe DiMaggio.

During the flight, Russ told the famous centerfielder all about our son. After landing, and while still on the tarmac, Joe stopped, opened his briefcase, took out a photograph of himself, inscribed, "Hang in there, kid, you can do it," and handed it over to Russ. Russ watched a single tear roll down Joe's face.

One compassionate droplet for an unknown boy's hopes and dreams—just one moment in a famous athlete's busy life—generated a glorious rebirth for our son.

Once out of his shell, Larry went on to play baseball, attend college, and marry. He now has children of his own. That photograph of Joe still hangs on Larry's bedroom wall and smiles down at him every night. Every night Larry smiles back.

LYNNE LAYTON ZIELINSKI

*You shall call upon me and I will answer you. I will be with you in
trouble. I will deliver you and honor you.*
—PSALMS 91:15

DOUBLY BLESSED

*B*irthing is a breeze. The toddler years, a cinch. I'm
convinced the most difficult stage of parenting occurs
when your teenagers begin to drive their own cars. When
my twin daughters, Angela and Linda, passed their preliminary
driver's education course, I found myself becoming overly anxious about potential mechanical problems and preoccupied with
the dangers young girls could face while traveling alone. They,
on the other hand, were full of the innocent confidence that
most young drivers possess.

Shortly after getting their permits, which entitled them to
drive only in Suffolk County, New York, the girls were invited to
a friend's house about forty minutes away. Worried about the
prospect of the girls having to travel on three different highways
to get to their friend's party, I tried to talk them out of going.
They were adamant about their ability to navigate the roads,
however, and I reluctantly agreed. Against my better judgment, I
gave them a map and anxiously showed them the routes they
would need to take.

Around 2:00 P.M., armed with a credit card, the map, and instructions to call home as soon as they got to the party, they

pulled away. An hour later I began to worry, and called to see if the girls had arrived. "I haven't seen them yet," their friend's mother told me, "but don't worry, I'll make sure they call you just as soon as they arrive." At 3:30, with the girls almost an hour overdue to their destination, I became frantic. Helpless to intervene myself, for the first time I called on my guardian angel and theirs to stay beside the girls and guide them home safely. My whole world felt on hold, and I could barely breathe out the prayer. But I nonetheless sought refuge in my imagined vision of angels swooping down and guiding them along a safe path. After another agonizing hour and a half, the phone rang and a timid voice said, "Mom?" I thought I'd explode, until I heard their story.

As they explained it, they got on the Northern State Parkway and never saw the sign for the first exit. They continued on the parkway west toward New York City, with Angela driving and insisting Linda read the map. Linda found reading impossible to do in a moving car and begged her sister to pull over. Afraid to pull over, Angela just kept on going! She drove right past the sign indicating they had entered Nassau County, a place where the girls' licenses were invalid, and proceeded on into Queens County. By this time, Linda became panicky. Years earlier, their grandparents had lived in Queens, and Linda knew they'd gone much too far. Yet, scared to stop, Angela continued driving.

By late afternoon, after driving through more than one construction detour, they found themselves on Grand Central Parkway. When Angela saw a sign indicating she was about to cross a bridge into New York City, she exited off the parkway instead. Now they were really lost! Their Suffolk County map did them no good, and the rush hour traffic in Queens had begun. Frightened and overwhelmed in the relentless traffic, the girls began to panic.

Spinning to look at the mass of cars around them at a stoplight, Linda noticed a red car with government plates pull up in the lane beside them. The driver, an elderly, grandfatherly-looking man, had white hair and glasses. Feeling safer because of the official tags and the driver who looked so kind, Linda rolled down her window and told him they were lost and needed to get back to the Northern State Parkway heading east. "Follow me," the driver said. "I'm going that way."

Driving slowly up ahead, he guided them from exit to exit, crossing the myriad highways, parkways, and boulevards the girls had mistakenly exited onto and off of in their fear and frustration. Finally back on the correct road, Linda and Angela followed the man until they recognized the signs they'd missed before at the correct turnoff. At that point, although neither girl saw him exit, they lost sight of the man and never saw him again.

"Linda, do you remember what time the gentleman pulled up beside you?" I asked after their return, recalling my 3:30 plea for angels to stay beside the girls and guide them safely home. "Actually, I do," she said. "I had just looked at my watch. It was exactly 3:30."

Coincidence? Perhaps. Naysayers would claim that angels are just a figment of our imagination. But I've heard that line before. "It must have been a figment of your daughters' imagination," the officer said when I called to investigate the good samaritan. "As far as I know, no red cars with government plates exist in the State of New York."

SARAH NEWBY

"Miracles come after a lot of hard work."
—SUE BENDER

THE POWER OF PRAYER

Y ou will never walk again. You will have to use a wheelchair." Unprepared for the doctor's grim prognosis, I heard his words fall heavily on my ears, numbing my soul. I have always been a devotee of St. Jude, patron of the hopeless and despairing. If I had never felt hopeless before, I felt hopeless then.

My catastrophic car accident had left me unconscious and in critical condition. I awakened to find both legs swathed in casts, the left one in traction to aid the healing of a broken hip and pelvis. While I had other serious injuries, my legs were my prime concern. Working as a special-needs teacher and "on the go" by nature, I couldn't imagine being confined, let alone an invalid.

Lying in my bed motionless and relying on prayer, I wondered how I could give my ten-year-old son hope that Mom would heal. He'd been cheerful on every visit, but I saw the fear in his eyes. Looking forward to having a totally handicapped mother and the implications of that were weighing heavily on his little shoulders. He needed the ray of hope that I would not be in a wheelchair forever.

Just maybe, I thought, I could use this experience to teach what to do when adversity strikes. But I wasn't just being altruistic. I needed something besides my physical healing to sink my Irish stubbornness into—it's that trait that kept me going through the toughest challenge of my life.

It didn't take me long to become impatient with my limited mobility and even with the pace the therapists were willing to go with me. I vowed to learn everything they showed me—and then some. Attempting to move on my own at night after the nurses' last rounds, I'm sure I broke every hospital rule. I needed to make things happen my way. And being confined to a wheelchair the rest of my life didn't fit into my plans.

At first, I taught myself to move from the bed to the wheelchair. I made tiny movements for weeks, afraid of falling, but more afraid to just lie in bed. I reached a point where my arms were strong enough to swing me into the chair. Getting out of the chair and back into bed proved more difficult, but I soon developed a method of grabbing the sheets with one hand and the traction bar with the other. I wouldn't win any gymnastics competitions, but it worked. I often wondered what the nurses and therapists would have done if they'd seen me struggling on my own.

Each of my "secret" therapy sessions began with fervent prayers to my patron saint of hope, Jude. My prayers allowed me to transcend the pain as I struggled to support my weight, and I noticed my movements becoming easier. Prayers for safety and patience eventually gave way to prayers of thanks and gratitude for any little progress I made.

Once sure I could return myself to the bed from the wheelchair, I began to tackle a walker that had been left in my room by a former hospital roommate. If the nurses noticed that the wheelchair and walker were not where they had left them, they were not saying anything. I wondered if a conspiracy of silence had developed: I wouldn't say anything about my secret therapy sessions, and they kept quiet as well.

Every night in my private room, as soon as I knew I wouldn't be interrupted or discovered, I would maneuver myself from the bed to the floor, holding on to the bed rail for dear life, and slowly putting my weight on my feet. After several weeks of these ever so difficult efforts, my strength and confidence continued to build. Now came the ultimate challenge: alternating and moving my feet one inch at a time.

I had dreams of striding briskly down the halls at school, playing dodgeball at recess, and driving again—grandiose dreams to be sure, but I knew one thing for certain: there would come a day when the wheelchair would be gone and I would walk.

It came time to share my accomplishments with the person most important to me. One night, before my son arrived for his regular visit, I pulled myself into the chair and stationed the walker in front of me. When I heard him greet the nurses at the station, I dragged myself up. As he opened the door, I took a few small steps. Shocked, he could only watch as I turned and started back to bed. All of the pain, the fear, and the struggle faded as I heard the words I had longed to hear, "Mommy, you can walk!"

I am now able to walk alone, sometimes using a cane. I am able to take public transportation to shop and visit friends. My life has been blessed with many milestones and accomplishments of which I am proud. But none has ever brought me the satisfaction and joy offered by those four little words spoken by my son.

MARTHA E. NICHOLSON

YOU RANG, MY DEAR?

*For years I had been besieged by almost every conceiv-
able respiratory illness known to humankind. Pneumonia,
pleurisy,* and bronchitis were a way of life. My lungs
routinely struggled for air, and my heart labored to pump life
into me. And I sabotaged these efforts by smoking and over-
eating.

I'd been especially close to my father. After he died, what little
sense of well-being I had vanished with the sudden onset of
panic attacks. Without warning I would find my heart racing and
be overcome with shortness of breath and paralyzing anxiety. I
grew despondent, put on even more weight, and cried out to my
now-deceased papa to help me. I heard no reply and spiraled
downward into complete despair.

My aunt, a psychologist, interceded on my behalf. She
coached me through my anxiety attacks and gave me the tools to
begin a long journey of healing. She said the anxiety attacks
were a gift, that they could teach me how to listen to myself. She
repeatedly encouraged me to get quiet, go inside, and listen to
my heart. For a long time, all I could hear was silence. Then, finally, I heard the sounds of a broken heart in need of healing. I
shed the tears that had been blocked with food and cigarettes. I
knew the pain of feeling separated from myself and Spirit. And
I quit smoking and began to lose weight.

One day as I sat listening, that small still voice told me that the
road back to wholeness was through prayer. I felt inadequate and
unsure about praying and mumbled half-formed prayers and felt

silly and embarrassed by my attempts. I decided to pray to my papa instead of Spirit. No insult intended to Spirit, but I felt more comfortable praying to one I knew better. I got out the program from my father's funeral service and read the eulogy written by my brother. He had included a wonderful quote from Edna St. Vincent Millay that captured the largeness of my papa's soul and the generosity of his heart. It read:

> *The world stands out on either side*
> *No wider than the heart is wide*
> *Above the world is stretched the sky*
> *No higher than the soul is high*

I decided to write Papa a letter. I wrote down everything that I could not speak. I told him how much I missed him, how my heart ached in his absence. I asked him to listen to my prayers and give them wings to send them where they needed to go. I cried out all my grief, all my aloneness, and all my sorrow until I was exhausted. I then fell into a deep sleep. The sound of the phone ringing awakened me. A woman from Houston whom I didn't know asked me if I had a neighbor named Paige who lived at the 306 address on my street. Bewildered and groggy, I replied that no such person lived there. She thanked me and hung up.

Just to be sure, I checked my Caller ID the next morning, certain that I'd dreamed the whole bizarre encounter. But I hadn't dreamed it at all. The memory of the call continued to nag at me as the morning progressed. For some unknown reason, I felt compelled to get the book I'd purchased the preceding day, entitled *A Treasury of Women's Quotations*. Acting on my intuition, I flipped it open, and it landed on page 306. The exact quote that my brother had read at Papa's funeral bounced back at me.

Awestruck by the simple yet profound power of Spirit, I sat down. Peace washed over me as I realized that I had, indeed, learned how to be still and listen. As suddenly as they came, the panic attacks were gone. For the first time, my heart opened wide, and a feeling of goodwill coursed through my body.

Now I pray with reckless abandon. I hear Spirit's voice, I recognize the sound of my own heart, and I never, ever screen my telephone calls!

MAGGI BOOMER

RYAN'S ANGEL

O ne warm October afternoon when I was writing at my computer at home, I heard a frantic knock on the door. My office was next to the front door, so the pounding sounded like thunder. "Lady! Lady!" yelled an unfamiliar woman's voice filled with panic.

I shot out of my chair and rushed to the door. "Come quick!" she said. "Your boy has been hit by a car!"

Ryan . . . My thoughts fused in a thousand dire images. It was impossible. He was playing in his room. He was right where any eleven-year-old should be. Safe.

Then I remembered he'd said he was going out on his bike to visit neighbors and to try to sell them the plywood Christmas yard decorations he drew, cut out with our jigsaw, and then painted. My budding entrepreneur had sold an entire "Snoopy" family to one neighbor though we'd lived in this area less than a year. Now he was making a trio of snowmen.

Visions of his sweet creations vanished as in my mind's eye I saw Ryan's body now mangled and lifeless.

Not even bothering to shut the front door, I took off running across our lawn and the empty lot that separated our house from the corner. It was a short distance, yet it was the longest span of earth I've ever crossed. Why wasn't I going faster? Why couldn't I see him yet?

I tried to scream his name but lost my voice. I felt strangely cold and numb. I couldn't feel my bare feet as they pounded over grass, then stones in the rough pavement. Suddenly, I remem-

bered the day he was born. His first day of school. His last birthday. His smile.

I knew my life would be over if he was dead.

"Please, God, take me. Not him. Take me. I'm ready. Let him
be alive. Let him be alive."

As I rounded the corner, I saw the huge Suburban and the
woman driver, a neighbor I'd waved to often but had never for-
mally met. She wasn't crying.

Her face held a stunned, incredulous look.

"Where is he?" I finally screamed at the top of my lungs.

"Mom!" Ryan's voice mercifully cut through the panic in my
head.

My eyes shot to him, sitting calmly on the curb. That same
stunned, glazed look in his eyes as in the eyes of the woman
driver.

"You're alive!" I burst into tears. Then immediately inspected
him for broken bones, internal injuries—surely something was
being overlooked. As I sat on the curb next to him squeezing and
poking his thin arms, I glanced at the Suburban.

There, under the back tires, I saw Ryan's twisted and crum-
pled bike. I realized instantly that something was very strange
about all this.

"What happened?" I asked the woman driver.

"He was riding his bike between the houses and those huge
bushes that hide the view of the street. But I never expected
to see anyone riding a bike out of those bushes. Before I could
even put my foot on the brake, he was in front of me. I hit him
head on."

I looked at Ryan. Not a scratch.

"Mom, it was the weirdest thing. I saw her, I knew I was going
to get hit and then . . . well, it was as if a huge hand just picked
me up and put me here on the curb. I didn't touch the car at all. I
sorta just flew over here."

The woman nodded. "He's so right. I know this makes no

sense. I heard his bike being crushed under my tires. I closed my eyes in horror. When I opened them, he was just sitting right there as you see him. Pretty as you please."

By this time, the police had arrived, sirens blasting, responding after one of the neighbors had placed the emergency call. The patrolman asked Ryan and the woman driver the same questions and got the same answers. Their story did not deviate in the least.

The officer scratched his head as he looked at Ryan's bike. "This is impossible! There is no way that bike could be twisted like that and your son not be dead. No way."

"Sure there is," Ryan said. "I was saved by my guardian angel."

The policeman was dumbfounded.

I smiled and winked at Ryan. We know where to look for angels and when to expect them.

So far, they've always shown up on time.

CATHERINE LANIGAN

V

BETWEEN US GIRLS

*"Believe it or not,
today offers you a hidden gift,
if you're willing to search for it."*

—SARAH BAN BREATHNACH

"I have enough to pay, play and give away."
—Bonnie Ingersoll

WHEN LESS IS
SO MUCH MORE

*I*t's over. *After more than a year of arguments, anger,* anguish, tears, and lots of second-guessing, my marriage of eighteen years ended a few months ago.

In difficult negotiating, rather than split my 401(k) retirement funds, I lost everything else instead. I lost my little yellow house with its blue shutters; my pretty pine bedroom set; the honey-colored oak dining set with sheaf-back chairs; my dishes, utensils, pots and pans, blankets, towels, and picture frames; the Eureka vacuum cleaner; patio furniture, potted flowers, bags of fertilizer, the nectarine tree I planted, packages of seeds, hand tools, nails, paintbrushes, the bicycle pump, and the beach umbrella. Over the many years it took to acquire all this, each item and its corresponding memory or story were left behind in a flash.

But I wouldn't trade this grocery list of possessions for the sense of peace that has finally cloaked my tired spirit. Now that the divorce and its cold, cruel legalities are final, and my emotions and attentions are no longer so frayed, it is as if someone hit the restart button on my synapses.

My five senses have suddenly intensified. Colors look dazzling;

food tastes delicious; scents smell wonderful; silk and flannel, cool water and warm hands feel good to my skin; and the voices of the people I love sound like music.

And with this reawakening comes gratitude for a new start—and for the houseful of worn-out, castoff possessions I so easily acquired in the whirlwind course of about a month. Many items were generously donated by helpful, concerned friends. Others were found on the side of the street with "Take Me" signs attached to them.

In the living room, an afghan covers the worn upholstery on the small piece of sectional couch I found (who knows what became of the rest of the couch?), and a blue woven shawl disguises a rather ugly rocking chair. My beloved books, which used to rest on solid oak shelves, now are roughing it on my new bookshelves of stacked bricks and plywood—home sweet dorm.

The dining room set is a round coffee table with four pillows around it that I hand-picked out of an apartment building Dumpster. I washed and resewed the covers, and my daughters and I kneel on them like a Japanese family. None of the dishes or silverware match. Neither do the place mats and cloth napkins inherited from several sources.

In the kitchen, the refrigerator is harvest gold, bought at a secondhand store for $49. My used frying pan lost its nonstick coating at least 500 meals ago.

My two daughters, who divide their time evenly now between two houses just a block apart, sleep on hand-me-down frameless mattresses. I covered the warm but stained garage-sale comforters with new cotton duvets, and the girls hung up their posters and school artwork and set up their critter cages to complete their bedroom.

There's joy in this mishmash of throwaways. These possessions have stories, but they are not mine. There's no emotional attachment; I could toss them as easily as I found them. There's a freedom in that. And it's all I need right now.

Did I decide to leave the marriage lightly? No way. But having lived under a marital roof of joyless rigidity, barbed negativity, and frequent criticism, without any hope of improving, I realized I couldn't live in that loveless environment any longer. I'm grateful for the chance to be a role model to my two daughters. I know they will slowly begin to understand that staying in an emotionally abusive relationship isn't healthy.

Suddenly, I see choices, possibilities. I'm nearly giddy with anticipation about what direction to take my life in. I can travel to any country, learn any language, or join any club. I can think my own thoughts and then bounce them safely off close friends. I can dance in the street, sing at the market, burp in a restaurant, giggle in church, eat chocolate in bed. I can leave dishes in the sink for two days. I can acquire brand-new possessions—or not. They seem so unimportant at this point.

It's the strangest feeling: I'm in debt up to my earlobes with legal fees and now must struggle weekly to live within the confines of a single-income household. I've lost everything I ever bought in the past eighteen years. Yet I feel rich. This is not just Pollyanna prisms-and-glad-games sentiment. I'm beginning to understand how regaining control in one's life offers a wealth beyond measure.

It's really not so awful losing so much. My spirit has just landed a windfall.

KARIN ESTERHAMMER

THE REUNION

he girls were getting together again. I greeted the invitation to a reunion with my friends from high school with feelings of apprehension as well as anticipation.

We had been closer once. Some members of the group moved away, but seven of us had managed to stay together all through high school. Even though we might've had different interests, we shared the same commitment. No matter what, we wouldn't follow fads or fashions—favoring comfort, we preferred flats when stilettos were in style. We watched *60 Minutes* more avidly than we watched *American Bandstand,* and enjoyed plays more than sock hops. Some of us even read poetry. We would stay true to ourselves. This commitment formed a bond between us and helped us survive our adolescence.

After high school, some of us got together, now and then, for lunch or dinner, sometimes bringing along the men in our lives. Eventually, family and career demands beyond our control made our times together rare treats instead of frequent habits. Months became years. We were slowly becoming strangers. This invitation provided a chance to rediscover the friends who knew me when I was most innocent and most vulnerable.

We met for lunch at a restaurant where my friend Marianne's daughter worked. How could a friend of mine have a daughter that age? I still felt like a teenager myself when I managed to look beyond the lies the mirror told.

We were all on time. Even me. Finding clocks superfluous

when we were younger, I never seemed to be at the right place at precisely the right time. The years had managed to work a few miracles.

We spent the first few minutes noting the most obvious changes in one another: new hairstyles, eyeglasses, pounds gained and pounds lost. After we sat down, there followed an obligatory exchange of wallet photos, inquiries about husbands, children, parents. As the photos passed through my hands, I began to wonder whether this meeting was such a good idea. Maybe there had been too many changes in our lives.

Some of us were married. Some were not. Some had children, others did not. We worked in totally different fields, lived in different neighborhoods, different worlds.

But, by salad time, I could see, despite the intervening years and the changes they brought, we were still the girls and very much our own women. Although our lives had followed different patterns, we still had the same values.

We talked about our own work and special interests more than home or family, because at this stage in life, we finally have time for ourselves. We were at quite an intense point in the conversation, trading experiences in our battle for equality in the workplace, when in came the waiter with balloons for Margaret. My friend's surprise birthday party reminded us more than ever that we were, after all, just girls wearing the masks of women.

Just girls, sharing birthday cake and chocolate mousse, moaning about the calories as we sang "Happy Birthday" to our friend and, at the waiter's request, to the party at a neighboring table.

For a moment, I caught a whiff of the butterscotch brownies we used to eat on Saturday afternoons in my friend Mary's kitchen so many years ago.

The time seemed right to bring out our treasured memories, hold them up to the light of our laughter, and examine them once again, like the rare jewels they are.

The past came to life. We relived a trip to the Sands Motel, a weekend rehearsal for adulthood where we giggled our way through dinner at the Polynesian Room of the old Edgewater Beach Hotel in Chicago and an all-night pajama party. The following day, we rode the bus home, wearing leis around our necks and world-weary expressions on our faces.

Memory followed memory. We relived afternoons spent playing the card game Spoons. We relived early parties with boys who used forks as weapons, catapulting pieces of chocolate cake across the room at us. Boys who played weird sound-effects records of bombs exploding that never failed to wake my baby sister. Boys who later danced with us to the theme from *A Summer Place*.

The past had never been more real. As memory played games with reality, I saw age as nothing more than smoke and mirrors after all. No matter what superficial changes time might bring, we would always be the girls.

MARY SASS

> *"You never get over bein' a child*
> *long's you have a mother to go to."*
> —SARAH ORNE JEWETT

THAT "KODAK" MOMENT

*L*ife is full of photo ops. I tried to be the good mom
and take pictures of all those "special times"—birthdays,
the prom, graduation, and so on—but I think I missed the
boat. It's funny how the most vivid memories I have in my own
mind of the years spent raising my two boys are not these kinds
of moments.

I don't remember birthdays much. After the first birthday for
the first child, the pictures all began to look alike, the memories
all run together. Proms, the big game, Christmas—these were all
great, and they're recorded for posterity in our photo albums,
but they are not the times I remember best. No, the really signif-
icant occasions, good and bad, the ones I remember best, are unfortunately not on film. I just have never been camera-ready
when the real events happen.

One of those "Kodak" moments caught me by surprise last
Saturday morning. At about 11:00 A.M., I took a ride into town,
and on my way, I decided to stop by my son Will's apartment to
drop off some of my homemade spaghetti sauce. Most of the
guys were at work except Will's roommate, Jeff, and my eigh-
teen-year-old, Curt, who still lives at home but had spent the

night at his brother's. "Curt's still asleep, and he doesn't feel well," Jeff told me.

I tiptoed into the bedroom and noticed a fan blowing directly on a mound of rumpled bedding.

"Curt?" I ventured.

From the middle of the bedding a voice croaked, "Mom?" Then a long pause. "Mom, I'm really sick."

"What's wrong?" I asked, going to the bed.

"I've been puking since early this morning. I even puked blood." That didn't alarm me. Curt has always thrown a little blood into his stories for dramatic effect. His head, eyes closed, emerged from the sheets, then dropped back down.

"I think I have to puke again." I wasn't born yesterday. I knew that sour smell that permeated the room. I asked him a couple of pointed questions.

"What did you drink last night?"

He hesitated, knowing how I felt about drinking, but realized denial was pointless. "A couple of beers."

"How much is a couple? A couple of pints? Quarts? A six-pack? A case?"

"I had about four beers. I swear, that's all I had." When Curt swears to something, I've learned to at least double or halve what he swears to, as the situation calls for.

"Then you went to bed?"

"No. I had the beer about midnight. I went to bed around two A.M. I felt fine," he groaned.

"How long did it take you to drink these four beers?"

"About an hour."

This conversation, translated into "Curt talk," told me that he had drunk somewhere between eight and twelve beers between midnight and 2 A.M. No telling what he downed before then. I realized that I would never have known anything about this if I hadn't made an extra-large batch of spaghetti sauce that morning.

I wanted to shake Curt and yell, "How many times have I warned you and your brother about drinking? How many times have you been told how dangerous it is—how it can suck you in? How dare you endanger yourself so carelessly after your father and I, who love you both so much, have invested all we have in you? After we've taken such care to keep you safe and healthy for the past eighteen years?" At the same time, I wanted to gather his rancid self into my arms and tell him about my relief that he hadn't ended up in the hospital or worse. I felt grateful that he would survive this lesson.

"You have a hangover," I said matter-of-factly.

"I don't think so. I feel awful, Mom. I must have the flu or something. It's really bad."

"It's a really bad hangover." I felt his head. He had no fever. I got a cold rag and put it on his closed eyes. "It's not the flu. It's a hangover. You've poisoned your system. That's what a hangover is. I hope you will remember this."

We sat there quietly. I stroked his hair. "Mom, I feel so bad I just want to cry. I'll never forget this. I'm glad you're here."

Definitely a "Kodak" moment.

I wish I'd had my camera.

LILLIAN QUASCHNICK

SECOND WIND

A pril days in Portland, Oregon, can convince you that winter will never end. A gray sky of drizzle after two weeks of downpours and puddles in the parking lots wouldn't give way. Looking at the city through the trees, I sat at my desk feeling a little sorry for myself. It seemed like I'd been giving out so much for so long. Juggling the multiple priorities most professional women do, I felt tired and discouraged.

I noticed the clutter on my desk: clean-up from a business trip piled high, stacks of articles, projects that needed attention, and an overwhelming list of phone mail messages. Slumping in my chair, chin in hands, I wondered what all this was worth.

The physical, emotional, and spiritual energy required in a field that called upon my professional singing, speaking, and consulting talents was exhausting. Giving out to others in an effort to make a difference had taken its toll. I wondered, *Does any of this really matter? Am I making any kind of contribution?* My thoughts turned to prayer. *God,* I thought, *You wanted me to do this, and I don't think I'm helping anyone. Maybe I'm just fooling myself!*

Morosely, I was plotting the career change I would inevitably need to make when the phone rang. The ring startled me from my brooding. A lyrical male voice, obviously Southern, said, "Hi, I'm Dan, and I'm calling from Texas. You don't know me, but I heard you sing in Japan."

Japan! That was years ago. It seemed like another lifetime. "Well," he continued, "I figured I needed to call you, because your music made a real impact on my life, and I figured you don't always get to know. I heard you sing at that school for missionary kids in Tokyo. During your concert, I was so moved, I knew then and there I needed to change direction. After your concert, I started studying my music so I could go into the ministry myself and touch others the way you touched me. I'm calling you because I just graduated from college this week and will be moving ahead with my dream."

"How in the world did you even find my number?" I asked, fairly stunned at these revelations from this friendly stranger on the end of the line. "Oh, I called around till I found it," he said. "Somehow, to call you right now felt real important." *Real important!* Little did he know!

We continued with our conversation, remembering that day years ago when I sang and spoke in Tokyo. I remembered feeling scared out of my wits singing for an assembly of high school kids. He remembered several of the songs. I remembered thinking it had probably been a total waste. He remembered it changed his life! As we exchanged addresses, I realized God had used the telephone to "reach out and touch someone." I don't always get to know whom I touch or how. I don't always get to know the impact when I give of myself. I don't always get to see the fruit of my labors. But this time, God used his impeccable timing to give me a precious gift—a call from a young man named Dan to give me a second wind.

KAREN HOWELLS

FISHING WITH GRANDPAPPY

❧⧖❧

Many *memories flooded back when I found this poem written by my grandpa in my childhood autograph book:*

When I am old, and my whiskers gray,
Bring out the lines, it's a good fishing day!

It reminded me that fishing with Grandpappy Roff meant more that just angling for "Mr. Big." Our adventures included locating a sunken island; seeing my first loon nest, complete with eggs; marveling at the mysteriously changing shoreline of that Minnesota lake where "floating islands" yielded to winds; and always plenty of laughter.

Mostly, I recall those sunny days spent at our cabin. Grandpa would dig the worms, row the boat, handle the anchor, and ration our snacks. I would dangle my hands in the water, watch the bottom deepen in the slant of the drop-off, and anticipate arriving at "our spot" beyond the bay. Grandpa said only because I baited my own hook could I go with him on these outings.

Then came the start of a new era, the first time a motor replaced our oars. We weren't yet tempted to use the mechanical speed for venturing into new waters, we were merely delighted to reach the crappie bed sooner. Not daring to hang my arms over the bow this time, I sat up straight. I smiled at the way the wind felt as it tousled my hair.

It's hard to forget a perfect day like that one! The crappies were bigger and biting on our cane poles faster than usual. We couldn't wait to show off our catch back at the cabin, where my folks and Grandma were waiting.

"Show them what we caught!" I proudly prodded as Grandpa cut the motor and we coasted alongside the dock.

Grandpa was silent. In his haste to get back to the shore, he had forgotten to pull in the net. Not one fish remained within the wire mesh basket!

The lessons I learned that day with Grandpappy:

1. Haste can make waste.
2. Don't tell your fish stories until all fish are present and accounted for.
3. Seize the moment, cherish the memory, and always tend to the nets!

LINDA G. ENGEL

LEG SHAVING 101

*I*n the spring of 1964, I turned thirteen and realized the reddish strands of hair on my legs could be clearly seen, trapped close to my skin by the stockings I wore with my penny loafers. I felt certain everyone else had noticed, especially the boys.

The Lawsons moved next door that same year. Until then I'd been the only girl in the neighborhood, and I quickly became friends with their fifteen-year-old, Rebecca Jane.

Becky and I spent hours in her room. We talked about poetry, or the characters of the latest book I was reading, Becky hinting at the unfolding drama, since they were all her recommended choices. But my favorite times of all were when she would sit on her bed with its new pink spread and delicately shave her legs using cream and a towel, right up to the edge of whatever pair of shorts she wore. We never spoke about the shaving. It felt like a great ritual that I was privileged to view. I curled my unshaven legs under me and watched, fascinated, as she rounded the corners and took the curves at her knees like a pro—and all without so much as a nick or a drop of blood. That summer I resolved to join the club, to be like Becky, to shave my legs.

All that July I watched Becky's shaving routine, eventually confident that I could duplicate it myself. One particularly hot night in early August, I announced my intentions at dinner. Becky planned to come over that evening to watch an old movie, and I wanted to surprise her. Now I would definitely be on her level. Now we would have more in common than the books we read.

Over the meatloaf, even though I knew the answer, I casually asked my mother where she kept her razors and shaving cream. My six-year-old sister shrieked, "Can I watch?" My mother calmly asked me if I knew at all what I was doing.

My father turned out to be Attila the Hun. This quiet, dark, brooding Italian father of mine turned a strange shade of gray, then promptly bounced his fist off the edge of the new dining room table, declaring that I was too young, and that no daughter of his needed to shave her legs.

He rarely yelled, preferring to leave that part of parenting to my mother, so I knew this must be a meaningful conversation. I bent my head over my meal and turned arguments over quickly in my mind. I decided to try the old staple, "But everyone else is doing it!" He didn't care what anyone else was doing, he only cared what I was doing, and one thing I was clearly *not* doing as long as *he* was the father was shaving my legs.

Only a roadblock. Fired up from weeks of watching Becky, I wouldn't be giving up on this quietly. I turned to my mother, and in my most polite voice, inquired at what age she had started shaving her legs. She thought for a minute, then didn't look at my father as she answered, "You know, I think at just about your age."

My father glared down the table at her, but my mother ignored him and rose to serve Danish Dessert, one of his favorites. I took this as an omen that I had chosen the right night—the subject dropped for the moment.

I cleared the table hastily after dinner and rushed my sister through the dishes. My father and Walter Cronkite were discussing the affairs of the world as I started upstairs, praying the Hun would be too engrossed to notice me. As I neared the top step, almost out of reach, he fired off his last volley: "Just remember: you do this tonight, you have to do it for *the rest of your life!*"

I had never made a decision in my almost fourteen years that would affect me for the rest of my life. I didn't even have pierced ears. I tried to shut out my father's warning. My stomach tightened as I ran bathwater and gathered my supplies. For some reason, I thought shaving in the tub would protect me from bleeding to death. I selected a new razor for the occasion, one I decided to keep on the window ledge to distinguish it from my mother's. I looked at myself piercingly in the medicine cabinet mirror, wondering if I would notice a change afterward. My resolve stood firm.

No one bothered me or came up the stairs as I carefully followed the Lawson method. "For the rest of your life" reverberated in my head as I carefully followed the nooks and crannies of my legs. I saw the thin trickle of blood before I felt the pain from the first nick. The second I saw coming and immediately stuck on a square of toilet paper from the little pile I had set out on the edge of the tub.

As I dried off, I was struck by the smooth feeling to my skin; the towel slid easily across the surface. I picked off the tissue and rubbed some of my mother's Jergens lotion across the silky surface, not caring when the nicks stung. My red badges of courage. With a recognition of my womanhood, I felt certain the face that looked back from the mirror looked older, somehow more mature.

When I came downstairs, Becky had a bowl of popcorn on the table, her offering for the evening. My parents had taken my sister for a walk around the neighborhood; the house seemed oddly quiet for such an important event.

We turned on the television, and I stretched my legs out in front of me as we waited for *Woman of the Year* to come on. I was certain that Becky would notice the sheen from my legs, as we munched popcorn and talked about Katharine Hepburn and her affair with Spencer Tracy while the movie started. I made it to the first commercial before blurting out, "What do you think?" as I turned my legs from side to side, light from the the TV bouncing off the smooth surface.

"What do I think about what?" she answered, genuinely puzzled. I took her hand and ran it across my left leg.

"Don't you feel anything . . . different?"

"I don't know—what am I supposed to feel?"

"My legs!" I told her triumphantly. "I shaved my legs!"

"Oh," she replied, turning back to Kate and Spencer, "doesn't everyone over twelve?"

MARNETTE K. GRAFF

STRAIGHT TO THE TOP

I finished ushering the last fan out of the ballpark in Arlington and turned to my supervisor. "I need to speak with the president, please," I said. The supervisor looked at me dumbfounded, so I repeated: "I need to speak with Tom Schieffer, the Texas Rangers' president." With a smirk he let out a hearty chuckle and explained that no one at my level talked with the president. Now I looked baffled. "Do you mean to tell me that the Rangers' president won't talk to one of his own employees, an usher?" I asked. Rolling his eyes, my supervisor rattled off a canned speech about how busy the president is, running a ball club and all. "Mr. Schieffer," my supervisor said, "trades players, signs sponsors, and evaluates ticket sales, among other things. He doesn't have time to talk to people like you." Now I laughed heartily.

Long ago I learned from my mom that if you have a good idea, you need to share it with others. I told my supervisor that I believed in taking those ideas straight to the top, with or without him. "Usually the person in charge is happy to listen to positive ideas that will uplift the spirit," I stated passionately. My supervisor folded his arms over his chest, and firmly informed me I could not speak with anyone, let alone the president. Feeling patronized, I whispered, "We will see about that" to the now empty ballpark.

The next day I sent my first idea straight to the top. My supervisor could perhaps prevent me from talking with the president, but no one could stop me from mailing my ideas to him.

I wrote Mr. Schieffer a note, explaining that I found the employee break room to be uninspiring, with its stark white walls. Six hundred seasonal employees took turns retreating to that room for a breather after they worked a number of scorching innings. Knowing a problem should be addressed only with a solution in mind, I created a number of vivid, inspirational posters designed to remind employees of the magic that comes from being a part of the Rangers franchise. Folding the posters and my letter into a large envelope, I addressed them directly to "Tom Schieffer, Texas Rangers President."

The next day, I arrived to find the break room buzzing with energy and laughter. My colorful posters adorned the walls.

Over the next few months, I frequently sent Mr. Schieffer poems I composed about the ballpark. My themes touched on the entertaining and compelling ritual of baseball: winning a game against our archrival, watching a father take his son to his first game, losing a teeth-clencher. I always signed the poems with my name and title: Marguerite, The Usher.

Late that summer, I arrived to work one day and received my daily assignment: I would be working in the owner's section. That bright sunny afternoon, I passed Mr. Schieffer's seat. "Marguerite, The Usher," he read from my name tag. "Are you Marguerite, The Poet?" Laughing, I confessed and explained that I had many ideas he might like to hear, and could we arrange a meeting? With a smile, he quickly agreed.

Several meetings later, Mr. Schieffer expressed his appreciation for my positive attitude, hard work, and inspiring ideas. He then asked if I'd like to "go straight to the top" and offered me a position as his executive assistant.

This past year, Mr. Schieffer and I have shared many ideas

while working together to create a positive, upbeat attitude at the ballpark in Arlington. When anyone shares an idea with me, regardless of whether they are an usher or a vice president, with a bold smile I tell them to go *straight to the top!*

MARGUERITE MURER

MAGGIE

I watched the old woman struggle down the sidewalk, her shoulders hunched, her back bent. She lurched awkwardly behind her walker, and as I approached, I saw her lined face and thinning gray hair. A teenager on a skateboard zipped by, exuding youth and vitality. "Look out," he yelled as he brushed against her. The old woman turned her head away in anger, but I saw the glint of tears and the lost look of the old and unloved. And I thought of Maggie.

I never knew Maggie's age or what kind of life she'd had before I met her. Certainly, she bore the marks of a long, hard life of ill treatment, and she had a certain way of flinching whenever somone moved suddenly.

I hadn't planned to bring Maggie into our lives. I took the children to Valean Farm to look at donkeys, not buy one. But one look into the dark-lashed lustrous eyes gazing with childlike curiousity into mine undid all my resolve. I wanted one.

We chose a lively colt whose soft muzzle poked inquisitively into my pockets, looking for a treat. Small and neatly built, Lexy stood no higher than my shoulder.

"She'll want a companion," said Val, the owner. "Donkeys don't like to live alone."

My face must have shown the dismay I felt. If one donkey stretched our budget, what would two do? "I don't think we can afford two," I said with a lump in my throat, mentally bidding Lexy goodbye.

"Well, I can see Lexy'd have a good home with you. Tell you what I can do. I have an old donkey here, too old for driving or hauling anymore. I took her on a trade and to tell you the truth, she's not much to look at. Can't get anyone to buy her, and I don't want her. But she has a gentle nature, and if you like, I'll throw her in with Lexy. She's over there."

I followed Val's pointing finger. A gray donkey stood alone, aloof from the other donkeys still crowding around us. Even at a distance, I could see that her coat was rough and patchy, with dark skin showing through here and there. "Don't mind the coat," continued Val. "She has a touch of the mange, but it'll grow back in soon."

We walked over to her. With coarse hair, sparse lashes, and ears that were scabbed and black from the mange, she looked even worse close up. She had a heavy build, with none of the grace of the other donkeys. She didn't look up as we approached, making it patently clear that she had no interest in us.

"Her name's Maggie," said Val. "She's broke to ride and she doesn't mind the saddle. Here, I'll show you." Val pulled a saddle off the fence and strapped it on Maggie. Maggie stood quietly, still not looking up. "Hop on." Val lifted up my son Nathan, plopped him on Maggie's back, and slapped her rump. Maggie walked a few paces, looking neither to left nor right. "See?" said Val. "Gentle as can be, and nothing spooks her." Maggie turned and came back toward us. For a moment, our eyes met.

And in her eyes I saw resignation and despair. Maggie knew that she wasn't lively and young like the rest of the donkeys around her. She knew that she wasn't wanted or desired, that she had no beauty or grace. And she knew that she was going to spend the rest of her life handed from one uncaring owner to another.

I walked over to her, put my hands under her grizzled muzzle, and lifted up her head. "Maggie," I whispered, looking into her eyes. "You're coming home with me. I'm going to give you a warm barn with lots of hay, fresh water, a green pasture, and an apple tree to give you shade on hot, sunny days. And I will take care of you for the rest of your life."

Maggie and Lexy arrived the next day. Lexy bounced out of the trailer and galloped up and down the fields, exploring every nook and cranny of her new home. Maggie walked over to the corner of the barnyard and put her head down. I understood. She'd been disappointed so many times before in her life. She knew better than to trust the whispered words of a stranger.

It took many months before Maggie allowed herself to enjoy her new life. She eventually came to have her favorite spot under the apple tree, her own corner of the pasture where the new grass grew tallest, and her own place in the warm, hay-scented shelter of the barn. Maggie learned to be loved—to lift her head for a special scratch under her pendulous lower lip, to lean gently against my side so that I could slip an arm around her neck, and to nuzzle in my coat pocket for the special treat she knew I always carried. She looked up at the sound of my voice, and in her own cumbersome way, galloped down the side of the hill to meet me. She joyfully brayed a welcome through the barn when I appeared in the mornings, and snuffled a wet goodnight into my ear as I closed the door at night.

Maggie knew she was loved—not for how she looked or for what she could do, but just for being Maggie.

She died in the spring six years after she came with us. She died in her corner of the pasture, with a wisp of new green grass in her mouth. She died quietly, without fuss, as she had lived her life. But in a departure from how she had lived most of her life, Maggie died loved.

For the old, the unloved, and even the unlovable, Maggie is my reminder that love is a one-way flow until the heart learns to trust.

PATRICIA WILSON

VI
A MOTHER'S IMPRINT

"Success is never a destination—it's a journey."

—Satenig St. Marie

TWO CRABS

*P*ut *two crabs in a pot and they climb all over each* other trying to get out. I'm not astrologically minded, but I've never been able to ignore the fact that Mom and I are both Cancers with birthdays one day apart. As long as I can remember, we've been at odds. We're separated by 1500 miles of ocean, different climates, two cultures, and a five-hour plane ride in cramped seats, yet we still manage to pinch each other. Usually, a phone call was as close as we got to a real visit. We talked about her animals or my kids, anything but each other—our personal lives were forbidden ground.

Then one year we had a difficult falling-out and didn't speak to each other. The phone calls stopped entirely. Forgiveness was something we both decided we could live without if it meant an apology.

During that year the bad days looked like Norman Rockwell gone bad. I rocked, but instead of reading the *Saturday Evening Post,* I rolled it up and beat pillows while I cried. I sat by the fire and wrote in my journal, then burned what I had written. I shut myself in my daughter's closet with her dirty clothes and Barbies and screamed until I was hoarse. I drove only back roads so no one would see me talking to myself. On the good days, I meditated. I sometimes visualized Mom in a healing white light. Most of the time, though, I saw emptiness.

In spring that year, I went to Mexico on a church retreat at a Benedictine monastery. A straw cross hung on the white cement-block wall of my room. A bare bulb dangled over two twin beds.

Hot pink bougainvillea out the east-facing window provided a bright spot. At nine the first morning, I sat on the slate floor of the open-air chapel with fifty other people, listened to the retreat leaders, and wondered why in the world I'd come. On the third day, I began to cry during a meditation and couldn't stop.

"What's the matter?" Alan, one of the retreat leaders, asked.

"Noth-ing," I choked out.

"Why don't you come up here?" "Up here" being the front of the room. I shook my head no. I've always had an aversion to up here. *Self-revelation was a mistake. I'd be fine. Really.* Fifty people waited. Alan and the other retreat leaders, Mary and Charley, weren't moving. Everyone sat watching me. My head said let's get out of here, but my body wound up center front.

"Pick someone to be your mother," Alan said. I picked Mary because for some strange reason, she intimidated me most. Mary and I sat face to face on the slate floor, legs crossed, and we role-played—Mary the mother, me the daughter.

"What is it you want to say to me?" she asked. My sinuses dripped. After all these years, I had an opportunity to say anything I wanted to my mother and all I could say was, "Is there any Kleenex?"

"What is it you want to say to your mother?" Mary asked again.

I wiped my nose with the back of my hand and took a jerky breath. " 'All that's happened doesn't matter, and I'm sorry I hurt you. Can we start over from here?' " Mary took my hands and locked her eyes with mine.

"Your mom loves you," Mary said. "Every mother makes mistakes and has her own pain, but that doesn't mean she loves her daughter any less."

Someone shoved a box of tissues in my lap, and even after I wiped my eyes, my side of the story seemed fuzzy. I remembered childhood trips to the Dairy Queen, just for me. The way I never could catch Santa or find any presents before Christmas, the way Mom talked Dad into letting me go to boarding school, even though Dad had been dead-set against it. Tender memories began filling that empty spot deep inside me.

I returned from Mexico, right before Palm Sunday. In the spirit of Easter, I focused my meditations on release and renewal. During one meditation, I pictured Mom's surprise as she received thirty-five yellow roses, one for each of my years. The enclosed card read, "Here's to the first thirty-five years. Let's start the second thirty-five from here." It took three days to remember to stop at the florist.

On Easter I thanked God for all my relationships and asked for healing. No sensations of rapture, white light, or weightlessness overcame me. The signs were much more subtle. What I noticed was that I stood taller after church. My shoulders were closer to where they should be, not wrapped around my ears, and the stiffness in my lower back, the stiffness that kept my gait short and tight, had loosened.

The next day the red light on my answering machine flashed. It took me a minute to recognize Mom's voice. Her soft-toned message ended with "Call me."

I flew out two months later to wish Mom a happy birthday. We hugged and cried, for ourselves and each other. Ocean still separates us, and we still talk mostly about her animals or my kids, but we don't pinch as hard or as often, and I've come to appreciate sharing the same kettle.

BURKY ACHILLES

"The finest inheritance you can give a child is to allow it to make its own way, completely on its own feet."
—ISADORA DUNCAN

COMING HOME

My daughter Jill had emerged from her teenage years with a bit of rebelliousness and a great deal of independence. Not a bad thing altogether, but at the time I was not always happy with her choices and mindset. She became engaged in her mid-twenties to someone my husband and I could not easily imagine referring to as "son." We wondered whether this relationship was born out of her need to prove to us that she was, indeed, "her own person"—or was genuine. Like most parents of young adults, we were blinded by our overwhelming desire to see our children happy.

A few months after they got engaged, they announced that they would be moving from California to Texas so that Jill's fiancé might take advantage of a career opportunity. We were made to understand that like it or not, the decision was final and not open for discussion.

We tried in vain to understand the wisdom of their thinking, but inevitably we were left with a strong sense of futility as the day of their departure drew near.

We pulled ourselves together as we said our goodbyes, all the while holding back the fear and concern in our hearts. After a final hug, I watched them walk out the front door with nary a backward glance. I didn't walk outside, because I didn't want to see them drive away. I felt my husband put his arm around my shoulders as the tears I'd been holding back finally began to flow. I looked up at him and searched his face for answers. "Do you believe there really is a job waiting in Texas? Will they be okay?" My husband nodded his head affirmatively as he closed the door, but the sinking feeling in the pit of my stomach told me that he was just as worried as I was.

My fears began to escalate as the days passed without a word from them. Friends tried in vain to console me, but no one except our son Jeff was able to make any sense of what was happening. His words went straight to my heart as he repeated them again and again. "Mom, you have to let it go and let Jill stand on her own two feet. She has to handle this one on her own. Didn't you always tell us that falling down can often give us the opportunity to rise to our greatest heights?" he asked.

Yes, I did believe this with all my heart, and now it was time for me to do what I always do when my vision is obscured. I needed to demonstrate my own faith by asking for divine guidance. It was time for me to dismiss the fear that was distorting my thinking and holding me captive in this difficult situation.

I sat in silence for a long time after Jeff left that afternoon. My thoughts turned inward as once again I asked to be shown the way out of the darkness. I prayed that the greatest good might come from this situation and everyone concerned might benefit from the outcome. As I began to release and let go of my personal will, I slowly felt the gentle awakening to the truths I needed. I realized that Jill was not lost to me but had to find her own way home. She was strong, and I knew she had been given the tools to turn a situation around if it wasn't working. I just needed to have the faith in her that I had somehow misplaced. I retreated further into the silence and finally began to feel a comforting peacefulness sweep over me and fill up all the empty spaces within my heart.

A few days later, I was aroused from a deep sleep by the persistent ringing of the phone. I reached for it and wasn't sure whether I was dreaming or awake, and then I heard, "Hi, Mom, did I wake you? I'm sorry but you usually go to bed so late, I thought you'd still be up. I just wanted you and Dad to know that we are okay and to give you a phone number where you can reach us." There were suddenly so many questions I wanted to ask, but I held back and let her tell me whatever seemed most comfortable for her to share. We said goodnight, and reluctantly I put down the phone as I acknowledged my gratitude and gave thanks once again for divine guidance.

She didn't call again for a while, but a few months later she gave us the news that she would be coming home, and within weeks they arrived back in Los Angeles. It seemed as though an eternity had passed in those few short months—a lifetime of awarenesses and realizations had been experienced. Jill came to the house alone and very matter-of-factly told me that she had broken off the engagement.

I listened carefully as she shared what was comfortable for her to speak of and dismissed the rest. I think we both understood the necessity of letting go of whatever we might not understand. With a sigh of relief, I acknowledged once again that life has so much to teach us if we would only be silent and listen to the sweet voice that takes away our darkness and moves us into the light.

Jill got married to someone else three years later. She gave us a wonderful son-in-law named Charlie, who seems to delight in calling me Mom.

TERRY COHEN

TIMOTHY'S LEGACY

My son, *Timothy, was born by c-section on a cold and snowy December night.* I barely heard his first cry before doctors whisked him to the neonatal unit.

Timothy weighed less than four pounds, brought into this world early when my body could no longer nourish him. At first, I could only reach into the incubator and gently touch his tiny hands. Two days later, I was allowed to hold him in ten-minute intervals while he clung to life.

One week later, Timothy developed further complications. His patent ductus, a heart valve that naturally closes at birth, had reopened. They rushed him into open-heart surgery. Family and friends came, and sat and prayed with us. He made it through the surgery, only to contract spinal meningitis. While a real fighter, Timothy died after only two and a half months with us.

Always focusing on how to solve Timothy's next medical problem, we didn't stop to think his time with us would be so short. All my life, I dreamed of being a mother. Heartbroken with the death of our beloved first and only child, I lost all purpose in living.

After grieving intensely for over a year, eventually I learned that I needed to fight for my well-being just as Timothy had fought for his life. And to love a child, I had to risk the potential pain of letting him go. So we attempted to create a new family— to no avail. I wondered if perhaps I wasn't meant to be a mother at all.

I poured myself into college courses, thinking we'd live childless. Yet, after receiving my bachelor's degree, summa cum laude, I continued to feel empty and lost.

When my sister's close friend adopted a baby from Korea, I got to hold him at my nephew's birthday party. I hugged him tightly, then passed him on to my husband, Brian. This beautiful, healthy baby boy became an instrument, planting in us a seed of hope.

Although we were apprehensive about adoption in general, a power greater than ourselves moved us forward. Our faith and hope prevailed. Within days, we began the lengthy Korean adoption process, filing paper upon paper and exposing our lives completely with the anticipation we'd have a baby to love.

The adoption process became a "seventeen-month pregnancy," the waiting almost unbearable. Twelve months passed before we knew a baby boy would be ours. On the eve before Mother's Day, we received a phone call from Korea that would forever change our lives. Our sweet precious boy had come into the world on February 23. Timothy had passed away on February 26, three years earlier.

Ironically, he, too, had a heart murmur from his patent ductus. Our pediatrician at home told us most patent ducts heal on their own. Although panicked on the one hand, we began to view the similarities of our sons as a sign. Like a crack in our protective armor, we had an opportunity to walk through our fears of losing another child, not always know the end result, and learn to risk again.

A week later, I opened the mailbox and saw a letter from Korea. Closing my eyes, I said a silent prayer, then tore open the envelope. The letter gave a health update: Our son's patent ductus had closed, and no heart murmur could be detected!

Two months later, carrying a diaper bag that had been packed and repacked a number of times, we drove to the Detroit Metro Airport. I wanted to believe that I would see my new son soon, but my mind raced. *What if the plane crashes before I see him? Will there be a mix-up at the last minute?*

With one anxious step at a time, Brian and I walked to the arrival gate. Just like an expectant mother, I could already feel the unconditional love flowing toward my new son.

I choked up as the arrival doors swung open. Years of waiting had taken an emotional toll. Passengers and onlookers, sensing a special moment, stopped and watched as I screamed and ran forward to take my son.

My heart pounded wildly as I held him close to me. My motherly instincts kicked in immediately, just as they had with Timothy—whose presence I could feel. I counted fingers and toes and began to tend to my new baby's needs.

Today Christopher is eight years old. He has surpassed all our expectations and fills our lives with joy. In the midst of everyday tasks, I know my purpose in living.

Five years ago, our new daughter Katherine joined us as well on a very cold and snowy December night. Like Christopher, she arrived from the other side of the world to complete our family. I could feel Timothy smile down on us again as we took this small, cuddly bundle home.

KATHY ADATTE OTT

I DON'T MIND WAITING

I don't have children of my own, so I appreciate opportunities to nurture other people's children from time to time. When I began volunteering at the children's hospital downtown, I knew I had come to the right place. The neonatal care center where I go on Thursdays is an extraordinary setting where nurses and doctors daily perform near miracles on very sick and very tiny newborns. It is a place of many joys and many sorrows all blended together in muted rooms painted yellow, pink, and light blue. For every computer screen charting blood oxygenation levels and heartbeat, for every gray tube connected to cold metal and flashing red lights, there is a tiny infant in need of twenty-four-hour care. The place is the essence of sophisticated medical technology, but stuffed animals and flannel baby blankets abound.

As a volunteer, I try to help the nurses out by holding and feeding babies. Feeding without the help of a tube or some surgical intervention is one of the aims of the care center. Babies who are "feeders and growers" are babies who are on their way. Babies who are so premature and underdeveloped that they can't yet coordinate the complexities of sucking, swallowing, and breathing in the right order can take hours of patient love and coaxing. Most of the nurses I have met wish they had all the time in the world to work with a special baby, but this is not the reality of modern hospital care. On any given week, there may be up to thirty babies in the center. In addition to the human touch and bonding that is the foundation for the infant's brain development, nurses must fit in updating the computer, keeping accurate chart notes, performing medical tests, and responding to emergencies.

The first time one of the nurses handed me a drug-addicted baby to feed, I felt my body's sensory system switch to red alert. I knew instantly, even before the nurse gave me some carefully worded instruction, that something was terribly wrong. I had heard the baby's high-pitched cry from several rooms away and it made me shudder. When I took him in my arms, he didn't mold comfortably there, as most babies do. This little boy had wooden-like limbs and a tiny ramrod spine, which arched up at my touch. He trembled from head to toe and chewed violently on his own hands.

This baby had come into the world addicted to methadone, which his mother took as part of a treatment for her heroin addiction. The methadone, a drug with a long half life, which is stored in the fat cells of the body, would make his withdrawal more prolonged depending upon factors such as the mother's dose and metabolism—up to twelve weeks or more. The withdrawal symptoms had begun a few hours after his birth.

The nurse instructed me gently and carefully that the baby was easily overstimulated. All the usual things that might calm a "normal" baby would not work for this boy. He simply could not process any complex combinations of stimulation, like my voice and my touch at the same time. We wrapped him up tight so that his limbs could not flail around, and I moved to a darkened area of the room clutching his bottle in my hand and hardly breathing. I thought that he would probably take the bottle quickly—he was supposed to be a good feeder—and then continue to cry, but he surprised me.

Instead of taking the bottle right away, he took only a small amount, stopped, looked up very briefly, then fell hard into a deep, fitful sleep. When he woke up, I continued to cradle his head very gently but firmly, and he fed again. Then he slept again. This pattern went on for some time.

I gazed at his face. He would be a handsome boy, with smooth skin and fine, even features. I wanted him to have the same chance at life as any other baby. It occurred to me that even with the powerful stress on his body, he was just trying to maintain control of his existence in any way he could.

As I studied him, I wondered about his future and the hopes and dreams he would have as he grew. And I thought about this eating-and-sleeping pattern he chose with me. Is this method of eating when he wants and sleeping when he wants the first experience of independence he has known since being born? Is there a seed of free will here, or will the legacy of the addiction predetermine aspects of his future?

Silently, I made a wish. I wished him freedom from the addiction that overshadowed his first few days and weeks of life. I thought to myself, *Perhaps I can give him a taste of freedom now—a space to exercise a small amount of control.*

The room remained still. In little nooks and crannies, nurses fed other infants. Behind a movable screen, one of the nurses trained a new mother how to breast-feed, and their amiable chatting and laughter made me smile.

Another nurse approached. "If you'd like, you can put him down now. We have a shift change coming."

"If you don't mind," I said, "I'd like to stay with this little guy for a while. He is taking his time finishing this bottle."

"At the rate he is going," she smiled, "it may take several hours."

"That's okay," I said to her. "I'll wait."

Susie Troccolo

IN HONOR OF MOM

I lost Mom in April. Five weeks later, the week before Mother's Day, I still turned corners expecting her to be there with a loving embrace and a word of encouragement.

I knew this first Mother's Day would be tough. A forceful, unsettled feeling stirred in me as the day grew near. Mother's Days past, I'd always honored Mom in some special way, and the thought of doing nothing this year seemed to deny her presence. I knew I had to do something to mark the occasion, but what, I didn't know. Then I realized it was okay to buy a gift, even in her absence. A gift to say "Thank you" for every wonderful memory; a gift to say "I cherish you."

Mom had a fondness for Precious Moments statuettes. At my request, my dad and fiancé accompanied me to the mall to browse. After a thorough search, I held up my choice with confidence, a palm-sized ceramic sculpture of a girl in a floppy sun hat, toting potted flowers and a packet of seed in her pocket. A gardener—like Mom, who planted seeds of love, compassion, and strength in me.

With my wedding only a month away, I felt much like a little girl. The little girl in my middle-aged body acted confused. I'd had a mother for forty years, yet felt orphaned. As my wedding day approached, fear overtook me. I didn't want to spend my wedding day focused on her absence rather than on the joy of our celebration.

Several friends said I'd be too busy to be sad. Others suggested a sedative. Nothing resonated until one of my mentors, a psychology professor, provided the wisdom and understanding I needed. "Don't deny your feelings," he said. "Your loss is so recent. Of course you wanted your mom to share your wedding day, so share it! Spend some time first thing in the morning visiting with her. Share your feelings and special news. Think about how she would have been involved during the wedding, and bring something of hers to the ceremony."

My throat tightened; my eyes teared. I now had a sense of direction. I took out the jewelry Dad had given me after her funeral. The ivory-white pearl earrings symbolized something borrowed, and the matching pearl necklace looked lovely with my going-away dress.

It wasn't until several days later—right before the wedding— that I glanced at the little statue, eyes uplifted, holding her flowers out toward me. I decided to accept her offering and brought the figurine to the wedding to represent Mom's spirit. I named her Alice, after Mom, and set her next to the guest book to help welcome our guests. During the reception, she offered her pastel flowers at the cake table. The photographer included Alice in several of the celebration photos. A dear friend took on the responsibility of escorting Alice home after my husband and I left for our honeymoon.

I still think of Mom often, especially when I open the wedding guest book or flip through the pictures and see Alice holding her own among the mingling guests. No sculpture could ever take the place of my mother, whose life and memory fill my heart. But if that memory ever grows dim, I have simply to run my hand along the shelf housing the growing collection of porcelain figures, one for each Mother's Day since her passing. They stand watch over my memories. Smiling at me, they echo her voice: "Carolyn, I'll always be with you."

CAROLYN MASTERS

IN THE DRIVER'S SEAT

I *look at you so proud and feeling grown-up in the*
driver's seat. A permit in the little purse next to you says
you are ready to drive a car. The question is, Am I ready?
Until your sixteenth birthday, it requires an adult to be next to
you. It requires me to breathe deeply, negotiate with my nerves,
and pray I won't wear a hole on the passenger's side from my
phantom brake.

My mind races with thoughts about you . . . about me (and
about the way you barely yielded at that last stop sign). How can
this almost-woman now driving my car be my baby? (Keep your
eyes on the road, don't play with the radio, and what's wrong
with the oldies station I had on anyway?)

I study your profile. Your baby features are but a memory,
your little-girl look all gone except for a few freckles that remain.
We're carrying on a conversation like two friends embarking on
an outing somewhere. But where are we going, you and I? You're
on a journey to grab the future, and I'm on a journey to learn
how to let go. (Good job on the left-hand turn.)

Where will your journey take you? Did we prepare you for it,
really? I listen to the inventory going on inside my mind like
some frantic mother double-checking a suitcase before she sends
her child off to summer camp: Hmmmm, let's see . . . did I give
you enough love? I have so much of it for you.

Knowledge? I've always been proud of you in this department.

Happiness? I wish I could give you an endless sum. Yet you are
in the driver's seat for this one. Your happiness will come from

the choices you make and the people you share them with. Choose wisely. (Any chance you'll choose to let me drive when we get to the expressway?)

Faith? Oh, sweetie! Will you realize life does take a lot of faith? I can almost hear your sweet little voice saying bedtime prayers while I tuck you in. Do you really know that the greatest strength and comfort besides your mother will come from prayer? The real challenge in life will always be keeping patient enough so your heart can be open to God's answers . . . even when they are not the answers you want to hear.

So much uncertainty comes with this precious package called life. I will not always be right next to you to give you directions and guide your turns in life or this car. (Are we almost there yet?)

I'm certain of a few things. Know there's not a moment, an hour, or a day that you will not have my love. Know that when you've lost hope, faith in God will bring you through.

I now feel the car stop and the keys being plunked quite comfortably in my hand. My daughter's eyes beam and say, How'd I do? I sing her praises (not literally sing—I was banned from that several miles back). I feel somewhat silly for being such a nervous wreck. She's earned my trust in so many ways, and now it's my turn to trust.

I say a quick little prayer of thanks to the Lord for the gift of this child (and for my car being safely returned to the garage). I can almost hear His gentle and reassuring whisper back to me: *Remember, someday as she leaves you, I will always be a passenger guiding her way. (You can stop braking now.)*

PEGGY KLINE

AN ENDING AND A BEGINNING

A *nagging feeling that I should travel to California to* *visit my mother just wouldn't let up. I ticked off the logical reasons why it wasn't a good time, and ran out of excuses. I knew Mom was doing okay after her stroke eighteen months ago, but I hadn't seen her recently. Since my father's death fourteen years ago, our relationship had been lukewarm to heated at times. My even-keel father had been a balancing force to my headstrong mother, and since his death the buffer he provided was gone.

My brother and I had shared much as the only two children in our family. We came from the generation where personal problems were hidden and never discussed. Though we didn't dwell on the past, we had both done our share of sorting out to look for understanding.

Mom came to visit twice a year, and I always cried when she left. She thought I cried because she was leaving; I cried because once again we hadn't closed the gap between us.

The stroke robbed her of the ability to talk, to write, and to be mobile. At first we hoped she could regain what she had lost, but over the months it became clear that she wouldn't. Mom chose to stay in a convalescent home instead of moving in with us. I sent cards weekly. I kept in touch with her friends, and together we managed the details of Mom's life. Not a great arrangement, but it sufficed.

When I arrived at the home, I met with the staff. Mom's condition had worsened, and they asked if I would order medical treatment she had refused upon admission. After we made sure she understood, Mom shook her head emphatically and let us know she wanted no part of any extraordinary measures. Tearfully, I went to tell the staff to make her comfortable, nothing more.

Needing to fly home a few days later, I knew that probably I wouldn't see her again. I brushed her hair, massaged her shoulders, and put lotion on her hands. I talked about things we had enjoyed together from time to time. My chatter sounded hollow, but I hoped it helped.

When I could wait no longer to leave, I prayed, *This is the last time I will see her alive. What can I say to bridge the gap? What can I do?* Immediately the words came: "Mom, we didn't always see eye to eye, but I always loved you." I desperately wanted a response. But whether the stroke took her ability to reach out, or she was unwilling, I'll never know. I left heartbroken that we hadn't reconciled. I'd done what I could, and yet that great distance remained.

Six days later, the call came from her friends. Mom had left this world peacefully, no suffering or struggle. The next forty-eight hours were a blur, and with fax, phones, and Federal Express, we managed to honor the funeral instructions she had left. Now that all the details were done, I bumped right up against my feelings.

I had always dreaded the day Mom would be buried. She had known many people, and their opinions of how I had interacted with her over the years were varied—none too favorable. I had gotten phone calls from people who didn't know we kept in touch. A few thought we should have taken her with us after her stroke, whether she wanted to or not. I wished I could have worn a sign to the service proclaiming, "I am not a troll." I don't like funerals anyway, and knowing that people who had misjudged us would attend made it all the more uncomfortable.

As the pastor spoke, a strange thing happened. Suddenly, I felt a pull to address the group. "Oh, no," I prayed. "Surely, Lord, you're not going to ask me to speak." Yet the feeling persisted and grew more urgent. I squirmed in my seat and tried to think logically. My family (especially my husband, who nearly grabbed the back of my jacket so I couldn't stand) feared what I might say. Wide-eyed and open-mouthed, they watched as I stood in obedience to God's leading.

I know exactly how David felt with a puny little slingshot as he faced Goliath. As I stood and turned to face the people, every trace of fear, resentment, and concern of what people thought vanished. Peace washed over me; and in the blink of an eye, God healed my defensive heart. Filled with love and appreciation for the ways in which these people had enriched my mother's life, I expressed my deep gratitude to them. I said they had stepped in and picked up the slack when we were so far away, and we were grateful. I told them that when I saw Mother eight days earlier, she was ready to go. I thanked them for their love and devotion to Mother through the years.

I honestly don't know all I said, yet I remember the complete freedom that poured through me as I thanked them for being part of Mom's life. Sitting down, I knew God had performed a miracle, and my life was profoundly changed.

Later, as I walked away from the cemetery, I felt no sadness. Only an incredible feeling of completion. I felt as if I had been a prisoner and now was released and walking in sunlight for the first time in years. Later, I learned that my brother had the exact same feeling.

I have learned much from the experience. I believe I am a better person; I know I have changed. Without fail, I now trust my own judgment. And I know, with the deepest certainty, that God can work miracles when we simply are obedient.

Oddly enough, I'm still not sad. I think of my mother talking, laughing, and walking in heaven's green fields after so many months of silence and confinement to a wheelchair.

She is at peace, and so am I. The hand of God closed the gap between us.

LYNNE SWARTZLANDER

VII
FAMILY FUNNIES

"A good time for laughing is when you can."

—Jessamyn West

THEIR GOOSE IS COOKED

I *could see the energy crisis peaking right in my* kitchen, one automatic gadget at a time. The countertops were beginning to look like the housewares department of an overstocked discount store just before a going-out-of-business sale. In fact, the only movable object that didn't require plugging in was my husband, Hank, who was self-propelled—especially when shopping for more gadgets!

When we first set up housekeeping, our only electrical contrivance was an automatic pop-up toaster. Hank loved it. At breakfast he'd gaze dreamily into the coiled slots, and when the bell dinged, he'd jump up right along with the toast.

Our next investment was an automatic coffeemaker. When Hank wasn't mesmerized by the toaster at breakfast, he'd get a kick out of watching the water turn golden brown as it dripped through the spout.

Then came the juicer. Its piercing whir provided a melodic counterpoint to the syncopated drip of the coffeemaker and the staccato pop of the toaster.

But the star soloist of the breakfast orchestra became our automatic egg cooker. The accompanying brochure proclaimed, "Boils eggs as simple as one-two-three."

The one-two-three part was right, but the process was anything but simple. It went like this: one, find a straight pin to puncture a hole in the small end of the egg so it can breathe while boiling; two, place the punctured end downward so it can boil while breathing; three, put a teaspoon of water around each three-minute egg (shorter or longer cooking time requires differing amounts of water).

Dutifully, I stored the appropriate measuring spoons inside the cooker, along with a supply of straight pins. On one occasion, however, Hank forgot to remove this paraphernalia before he plugged in the cooker. No eggs were served that morning, but we had enough sterile instruments to perform minor surgery.

We reserved the bacon cooker and the waffle iron for use only on Saturdays, Sundays, and legal holidays. Between the sizzling bacon and the sticking waffle iron, Hank didn't need the morning paper to keep him occupied; a baton to conduct our orchestra would have been more appropriate.

The day he brought home the blender was a real occasion. That blender blended, grated, chopped, stirred, ground, puréed, whipped, mixed, liquefied, and frapped (or so Hank reported, breathlessly).

Hank became so excited over having these ten choices for preparing food that he took a head of cauliflower and tried each speed, watching the blades go round and round. At last, the final product emerged: cauliflower frappe.

Our next three automatic wonders were a hamburger cooker, a hot dog cooker, and a peanut butter maker. Therein lie three more tales.

A hamburger cooker is great if you are all alone in your room and don't feel like walking to the local fast-food stand. But for feeding more than two people—forget it. By the time you get around to serving the third guest, the first is ready for seconds.

Nor has the hot dog maker exactly worked out. It holds six hot dogs, but the contraption cooks them at such speed that they undergo a kind of jet lag and shrivel up so that it takes two hot dogs to make one serving.

Which leaves the peanut butter maker. Now, all supermarkets offer smooth peanut butter, chunky peanut butter, and so-called "old-fashioned" peanut butter. Terrific! But our peanut butter maker produced only its own in-between variety: a jar of glob too thick for a milk shake but much too runny for a peanut-butter-and-jelly sandwich. So we stored the machine in the cupboard—for future reference.

One day, the inevitable happened. Hank brought home a machine that could do everything but plan menus and pay for the groceries: a food processor.

According to the pamphlet for our pièce de résistance, once you live with this "mind-boggling miracle of modern ingenuity," you'll wonder how you ever got along without it. "Mind-boggling" is right. A gadget within a gadget within a gadget. It came with nine attachments. One blade chopped and sliced vegetables, one grated cheese and chocolate, one ground raw and cooked meats, one puréed soups, and one made a mousse in a minute.

The idea of one-minute mousse turned Hank on. So he set about preparing it for dinner that night. His first problem was that while the recipe called for four egg whites, the food processor lacked an attachment for separating whites from yolks. It took Hank twelve eggs to produce the four clear whites.

Needless to say, as Hank was busy tending the eggs, the chocolate that he was melting scorched on the stove. It was the last baker's chocolate in the house, so we settled for burnt-minute mousse.

Each ingredient had to be mixed in the machine for precisely $12^3/_4$ seconds. I stared at my watch while Hank ran the processor, using all nine attachments. Victorious at last, he proudly spooned out burnt-chocolate mousse for four. Unfortunately, we had six to feed.

Counting cleanup time, his one-minute mousse took him one hour and eight leftover egg yolks.

This realization made something inside me snap. After Hank left for work the next morning, I carried all our gadgets—from pop-up toaster to miracle food processor—out the back door. I placed them in a perfectly straight line on the garage floor, right under the door frame.

I took one last look at the gleaming array of stainless steel, cast iron, glass, and Teflon. Then I stepped back purposefully.

As I pushed the button on *my* favorite gadget, the automatic garage door began to close, noisily, irretrievably. . . .

LOLA D. GILLEBAARD

HOUSTON, WE HAVE A PROBLEM!

My twin *four-year-old daughters recently began* their journey through the hallowed halls of formal education with their first trek to preschool. Sixteen bright-eyed kids with two incredible teachers were embarking upon a mission to study the mysteries of the universe—the theme of the year. Amid space creatures dangling from the ceiling and twinkling stars sparkling overhead, I kissed my little voyagers goodbye. Tears filled my eyes, and my heart pounded. I didn't feel the grief of a parent sending her children into an unknown galaxy, surrendering all control over exposure to otherworldly frights. What really struck terror in my heart was a more pressing nightmare: preschool snacks!

As a parent of two tiny astronauts, my mission was to supply nutritious snacks for the entire crew on two consecutive days every few weeks. Yikes! Our life is one of barely contained chaos—we can plummet into complete entropy faster than the speed of light. As a two-career couple, we can barely get dinner on the table, and now we have to supply snacks at a preschool that costs as much as my undergraduate college tuition!

Lacking proper orientation to the world of school snacks, we observed our predecessors. On the first day, James brought Goldfish crackers, apple slices, and grape juice—a worthy effort. The following day, Megan appeared with red grapes, graham crackers, and apple juice—another fine choice. The third day, my daughters complained bitterly that Allison brought more Goldfish and apple slices. Clearly, the snack became the critical component in gauging the overall success of the day's space flight.

The explorers vaulted into a whole new galaxy of snacks on the fourth day. Zach skyrocketed into celebrity status with his offering of chocolate chip cookies and milk. To compound matters, Zach had made the cookies with his dad, making them not only wildly successful but politically correct as well. The floodgates opened. Snacks of brownies, cupcakes, ice cream, and marshmallow pies all graced their spaceship.

The pressure really mounted when Brittany skipped in carrying a Tupperware container filled with edible aliens. Little creatures with Rice Krispie bodies, M&M eyes, and red licorice antennae!

My kids didn't even try candy until they were almost three. Before launching their career as astronauts, they had considered indulging in a single Hershey's Kiss to be a major event. What's a working, cooking-challenged, nutritionally conscious parent to do? Order freeze-dried yogurt from NASA? Disguise broccoli florets as Plutonium vegetation? Have my angels be ridiculed off the planet for these meritorious endeavors?

After much anguish, we put the girls in charge of their own snacks. We piled into our lowly earthbound vehicle for a trip to the space station refueling center also known as the A&P. My firstborn astronaut chose "pink juice" (alias Cranraspberry juice), poppy seed muffins, and raisins. She is surely the only pint-sized adventurer in any solar system who passionately relishes these treats. Her sister chose a NASA favorite: "granilla bars" as she calls them, orange slices, and a staple in any universe—water.

As I transported them to their space station, I knew that their snacks might precipitate a hunger strike by their fellow explorers. But they went boldly where few had gone before, delighting in the prospect of saving their friends from a nutritional black hole.

Two weeks passed, and their turn for snack delivery came

back around. Astronaut #1 declared that she'd take frosted Creepy Cookies with candy corn teeth and marshmallow eyes. She would top it off with Swamp Soda. Astronaut #2 lobbied hard for Slimeball Swizzle and cream-filled Martians.

Neither Mission Control Commanders nor rookie astronauts can fill a black hole alone. I'll have to abandon my job to focus entirely on the culinary requirements of little adventurers at snack time. Maybe chocolate-covered carrots will be next.

O. C. O'CONNELL

"Mothers . . . are basically a patient lot.
They have to be or they would devour their offspring
early on, like guppies."
—MARY DAHEIM

DOUBLE TALK

*C*onvincing my son Jeremy of the importance of a college education in achieving the "American Dream" has been a losing battle. Like most kids his age, he's star-struck and dreams of becoming a rap star or the next Michael Jordan.

Since he will be graduating from high school in another year, there's been a sense of urgency in my mission, and I never miss out on the opportunity to use real-life examples to illustrate how my college education has benefited me.

About a month ago, I treated myself by purchasing a new VCR and TV for my room. As I struggled with the instructions for about an hour after I brought it home, I stubbornly broke down and asked for Jeremy's help. In a matter of minutes, it was a done deal.

Everything was assembled and programmed because of his talent for putting things together. When he finished, with a smirk on his face and a great deal of satisfaction, he declared, "So much for that ol' college try!"

Jennifer Brown Banks

DUST TO DUST

Yesterday a vacuum cleaner salesman came to the door. I don't normally have door-to-door salesmen. I live about ten miles out of town, and you have to go over a canal and through three dogs to get to me, so I was really surprised.

The salesman looked to be about eighteen. He had a slight speech impediment and a haircut that made him look endearing, so when he said, "I get paid if you let me come in and do a demonstration. It'll only take twenty minutes," I decided, What the heck? My husband was out back within view of the house, and I was having a slow day anyway.

He dragged in a couple of very large boxes and proceeded to assemble this flashy-looking vacuum. I don't remember the last time I've seen a brand-new vacuum, but with all the chrome and gadgets, you kind of feel like you're watching the assembling of a nifty little sports car right in the comfort of your own home. When it was all assembled and strategically placed in the middle of my front room, it was breathtaking. It stood gleaming in the beam of sunlight streaming in my picture window.

Giving me a moment to get the full effect, he turned to me and said, "I need your vacuum so I can show you how superior this new model is to whatever you have." It flashed across my mind that it would really be great if I had, say, a brand new top-of-the-line vacuum lying in wait in my closet, something that I could whip out right then, catch the salesman off guard with, and challenge him with right there at high noon in the middle of

my front-room floor. I'd vacuum that smile right off his face. Instead I had to swallow my pride.

I went to the hall closet and pulled out my geriatric canister
vacuum. I hadn't noticed until now just how bad my veteran
looked. I felt guilty, as if I had just taken a good look at my husband and noticed for the first time that he was in the last stages
of some fatal illness. I pulled it out, its big swatch of gray duct
tape keeping its cord on, its right back wheel wobbling from the
time my son ran over its rear end after vacuuming his car. The
salesman quickly assembled my vacuum and began vacuuming a
small area of carpet over and over and over. This puppy didn't
stand a chance. I knew it wasn't cleaning the carpet too well. The
bag was probably still the one from the post-Christmas cleaning,
when I had vacuumed up about 50 percent of the pine needles
from our dried-up Christmas tree. I could tell because it was still
scenting the room nicely a month later.

When he finished, he carefully laid my vacuum aside like a
convalescing war veteran and turned his attention to his fancy
upstart. He flipped a switch and the floor began to vibrate. The
carpet came to life. It actually rose up off the floor to meet this
virile machine, like an eager lover. It was amazing. It lasted just
an instant, then the salesman turned it off and opened the air
vent. He pulled out a white tissue-like disk. It was a half-inch
deep with sand, dust, and cat hair. And he hadn't even moved the
machine. My jaw dropped. Here I was, peacefully going about
my business every day with this false sense of how clean my
home was, and it was actually filthy! I was living a lie! I might as
well be living in a log cabin with dirt floors!

Satisfied that I was duly impressed, the salesman then flipped
open a box full of attachments. There were the standard
brushes, but he bypassed these and pulled out this thing with
tines on one end. "This is a handy tool. It's for giving scalp mas-
sages and for grooming your pets." (I could see it now. Fire up
the engines! Here, kitty-kitty. How was your day, honey? Here,

let me vacuum your head.) Then he showed me how the same attachment could be used to change lightbulbs and unplug sinks. He showed me the shampooer, the overhead-fan blade brush, the round brushes, the long brushes, and the brushless attachments. The last attachment he came to was a needle-nosed gizmo. "This is a handy little attachment. It's for blowing up rafts." (In my mind's eye I pictured a bright summer day. Hey, kids! We're going up to the lake for the day. Load up the vacuum!) This attachment didn't seem like much of a selling point, but I was getting into the spirit of this.

An hour into his twenty-minute demo, the salesman began to get philosophical. It was time to talk lifetime investments, making wise choices, how life is too short to spend in dirt and drudgery, how the quality of merchandise is remembered long after its price is forgotten. Then he talked price. I talked disposable income. He talked value. I talked realistic budgets. He talked installment plans. I talked dinner plans.

He finally left. I walked across my now clean floor, wrapped up the cord of my battle-scarred vacuum, being careful not to pull the tape off, and tossed it back in the hall closet. I guess I could live with dirt. After all, life is too short and we're all in it together. Ashes to ashes, dust to dust (and then some).

LILLIAN QUASCHNICK

> *"More than Santa Claus, your sister knows*
> *when you've been bad and good."*
> —LINDA SUNSHINE

SUCCOR AND SPICE,
MY SISTER IS NICE

lthough my sister and I had our squabbles, I would be foolish to request a trade-in. I'm told that when I was an infant, my two-year-old sister would cuddle me and coo and insist on helping to change my diapers. Decades later, as I floundered between college and graduate school, she comforted me with food and shelter. Between those two stages of my life, I recollect only a couple of periods when my sister and I were foes.

When we were just kids in grade school, my sister broke her leg. By then, she was no longer interested in playing mother's helper. Instead, she literally threw her weight around. Whenever she wanted to exert power over me, she would swing her leg across my torso and pin me down. She was on the road to bullydom—not that I was the perfect angel. And then puberty! Her personality worsened as we grew closer in size and I began to wear her clothes without permission. Like hot salsa, her temper flared whenever she caught me in the act. Our relationship remained on the spicy side as long as I continued to snatch clothes from her side of the closet.

Then, of course, there was our ongoing feud over the dinner dishes. Whenever it was my turn to wash and her turn to dry, she would send half of the dishes back as dirty, whether they were or not. One night, I got upset enough to march into the living room and complain to my dad. Absorbed in a television program, he didn't really hear me, but he said "yuuup" to my request to throw spaghetti leftovers in her face. I did not hesitate. I raced right back to the kitchen and pitched that bowl of pasta dead center onto her nose. Then, just like in the movies, I smeared it all over her face.

The ultimate revenge for this kid sister! I remember feeling really "big" and satisfied for once. As for her, she was so shocked that she couldn't react. I really got her back that time—or else she just outgrew tormenting me—because to this day she has never retaliated.

Now, as adults, we treasure each other's company and friendship. We share similar wit and disposition, and often chuckle over events of our childhood. Somehow, we've managed to transform our shared experiences into lighthearted lessons that help us cope when the going gets tough.

For instance, she often advises me to "just throw spaghetti in their face" whenever I'm bothered by the way someone is treating me. Or if I just need to vent, she might advise me to "just go smash a cake to pieces," a reference to my reaction one day when she ate most of the icing before I had a chance to finish decorating a cake I had just baked. The layers weren't stacking well, the crumbs were smearing all over what little frosting was left to spread, and I lost it! I grabbed a spatula and pounded the cake to a pulp. Whenever I'm facing a frustrating situation, all I have to do is imagine my infamous mound of gooey cake crumbs and my perspective shifts.

Neither my sister nor I remember why we were laughing uncontrollably one afternoon while rowing our dinghy. Nor do we understand why we were oblivious to the only other boat at our end of the lake. When the two boats collided, our laughter only intensified. Simultaneously, we experienced amusement, embarrassment, and guilt. Perhaps because he wasn't laughing, the solo oarsman apologized first. I remember making a concentrated effort to respond. I wanted to apologize, but my lips, quivering with suppressed laughter, could barely form the words I needed. I finally blurted out, "Oh, no! It was part our fart." Needless to say, this blunder only served to increase our hysteria. And it brought a smile to our unexpected and surprised visitor.

Forty-some years later, we continue to crack up over this one. But this silly, slightly embarrassing experience has resulted in a powerful idiom of compassion and consolation. Whenever we utter that slip of the tongue on purpose, it's a sign of love and acceptance. Once, when I was agonizing over a relationship that was ending, my sister wisely pointed out that it was only "part my fart." Another time, I reminded her that a parenting predicament was only "part her fart," considering she had a husband.

Over the years, our catalogue of prized expressions has expanded. As our repertoire grows, the depth and quality of our relationship grow as well. I think we'd both agree that this much-cherished relationship, grounded in succor and dashed with spice, is "both our farts"!

DEBBIE PETRICEK

CONTRIBUTORS

BURKY ACHILLES works at a series of odd jobs to help support her family and her writing habit. She's the recipient of a Walden Fellowship and Soapstone Residency for Women Writers. Burky's working on her first novel, as well as a series of short stories about growing up in Hawaii. (503) 638-4100.

JENNIFER BROWN BANKS is a Chicago-based journalist, poet, and businesswoman. She has been a contributing writer for *Being Single* magazine since 1995, and has self-published three collections of poetry. Her articles, verse, and commentary have appeared in the *Chicago Sun-Times*, *Being Single* magazine, *Today's Black Woman*, Fireside/Simon & Schuster's *Chocolate for a Woman's Heart, Just for Black Men*, *Today's Chicago Woman*, *Chicago Defender*, and *Positive Connections*. Banks is the founder of Poets United to Advance the Arts. (773) 509-8018.

CAROLE BELLACERA is a writer living in Manassas, Virginia. Her fiction and articles have appeared in over 200 magazines and newspapers in America and abroad, such as *Woman's World, The Star, Endless Vacation*, and the *Washington Post*. Several works of fiction have won awards in contests, such as Columbia Pacific University's *CPU Review* prose contest and *The Belletrist Review's* annual short story contest. Her first screenplay, *Border Crossings*, was a finalist in the 1995 Austin Heart of Film Competition. The novel version of *Border Crossings* was published in hardcover by Forge Books in May 1999. <KaroBella@aol.com> <http://members.aol.com/KaroBella>

TANNIS BENEDICT grew up traveling all over the world as the child of Air Force parents. She and her husband, Brian Frankish, have a film development and production company, Frankish-Benedict Entertainment, in which they dedicate themselves to "stories of the heart." Her writing debut was a two-character play, *Timing Is Everything*, a romantic comedy produced in Los Angeles, where she lives. She also writes screenplays, short stories, and poetry, and has been an actress for over twenty years. After she lost a son, in 1996, her faith in God and the power of prayer have blossomed and illuminated her spiritual path. <tannisb@aol.com>

MAGGI BOOMER is married and works as a central supply distribution clerk at an area hospital. She is learning, through reading and meditation, how to live what she considers to be an authentic life, and she is currently studying the possibility of reversing her lung disease through alternative medicine and natural healing. (618) 465-5283.

JOY BOYD is a wife, mother, and motivational speaker. She believes in the "I Am's" and continues to utilize them in her workshops. She is currently studying for a degree in graphic design. (302) 836-1995.

DEBRA AYERS BROWN is the mother of an energetic third-grade student and is the public relations and development director of Savannah Technical Institute. She has won numerous national design and writing awards. The author of several inspirational and children's stories, she is currently working on a mystery novel series. Her husband is the mayor, which makes her the First Lady of Hinesville, Georgia. (912) 876-4617.

RENIE SZILAK BURGHARDT, who was born in Hungary and came to the United States in 1951, is a freelance writer. Some publications in which her work has appeared are *Angels on Earth, Mature*

Living, Fate, Cat Fancy, Midwest Living, Nostalgia, and *The Friend.*
She resides in Doniphan, Missouri. (573) 996-7750.

Terry Cohen enjoys writing as a means of self-expression.
She started writing as a young mother to entertain her children with humorous stories that were often read in the classroom. She wrote a two-part story for the TV series *Gentle Ben.*
She has owned and operated a successful antique store as well as
two gift and home accessory stores. Occasionally, she returns to
the classroom as a volunteer in her grandson's first-grade class.
She is compiling her life stories for an autobiography.
<Helowrld@aol.com>

Linda G. Engel resides with her husband and children in the
heart of the Minnesota lakes, where she was born and raised.
She earned her master's degree in communication disorders and
was a speech/language clinician and coordinator in public
schools for twenty years prior to the adoption of a son and
daughter. When not working as a freelance writer, she enjoys
fishing and other outdoor activities with her family. She is working on the completion of her first book, *Excuse Me, I'm Grieving.*
(218) 829-3433. <ssengel@uslink.net>

Karin Esterhammer is a columnist and editor for the *Los Angeles
Times.* She lives in Burbank, California, where her passions include her two daughters and everything German—language,
culture, history, and cooking. (818) 842-1852.

Candis Fancher, M.S., C.C.C., is a speech language pathologist
in a hospital setting. She integrates humor and "pleasure pause"
strategies to enhance patient care, communication, and healing.
Faith, family, and friends are her personal highest priorities. She
lives with her husband and best friend Dwayne, a pharmacist,
and her children, Chad and Jill, who describe her as being "spon-

taneously weird." Her Inner Sources seminars, "Staying Afloat in the Stresspools of Life," entertain, inform, and inspire participants to Stop, Notice, Act, and Create heart-to-heart connections. (612) 890-3897.

JACQUELYN B. FLETCHER works for *Minnesota Monthly Magazine* in Minneapolis. <jfletch@minnesotamonthly.com>

LOLA D. GILLEBAARD lives in Laguna Beach, California. She is a recipient of the Reader's Digest Writers Award, a professional speaker, and a past president of the Greater Los Angeles Chapter of the National Speakers Association. Her one-woman show, *Life's Funny That Way,* has been acclaimed all around the country. Lola is a humorist, an associate college professor, an author, and a corporate keynote speaker. She believes that laughter is the handshake of good communication and that humor in business is serious business. (714) 499-1968.

TAG GOULET, M.A., is a dynamic speaker who has helped more than 200,000 people commit to and achieve their dreams. A university instructor and newspaper columnist, she is the author of several books and *Recipe for Success,* an inspirational CD-ROM distributed in sixty-five countries. A specialist on "the power of commitment," Tag has been interviewed hundreds of times by media throughout the United States and Canada. She is currently writing *Courage to Commit,* a book about simple ways to create the life you want through commitment to yourself and your dreams. Call (888) HEART-24. <tag@heartpath.com> or visit www.heartpath.com

MARNETTE K. GRAFF, R.N., lives and writes in rural northeastern North Carolina, where she manages her husband's surgical practice. She teaches creative writing, writes a column for her local paper, and has worked as a script and medical consultant for television and movies. Holding a B.S. from St. Joseph's College on Long Island, N.Y., she has studied at Radcliffe, New York University, and the University of Iowa. Marnette is the author of screenplays, poetry, and short stories, and currently researching a murder mystery set in England's Lake District. (252) 943-9100.

DONNA HARTLEY is an international speaker, a member of the National Speakers Association, a change specialist, and a survivor of a DC-10 plane crash. Owner and founder of Hartley International, she has been featured on NBC, ABC, PBS, and The Learning Channel and in the *New York Times*. Her popular book, video, and audio training series is called *Get What You Want*. (800) 438-9428.

KAREN HOWELLS is a speaker, trainer, and consultant. She has worked for over ten years with major corporations such as Intel, Hewlett Packard, Nike, and Textronix in the areas of leadership, team development, and communication. Also a professional musician, she has sung with both the Oregon and Seattle Symphonies and frequently combines her business and performing arts experience to present information in innovative and inspiring ways for conferences and corporate events. Karen has also recorded two solo albums and is currently working on a third album, *Second Wind*. (503) 246-2929.

DEBB JANES is a morning radio personality and newswoman in Portland, Oregon. She's also a part-time teacher at Mt. Hood Community College and is working on several books. She's an environmentalist and a lover of the outdoors. In her spare time, she hikes, climbs, and fly-fishes in the great Northwest. She's also an avid gardener and a believer in self-development through awareness and spirituality. She lives with her thirteen-year-old daughter Kelsea.

MARLENE R. JANNUSCH, Ph.D., is retired after thirty-plus years of college teaching and administrating. This wife, mother, grandmother, educator, businesswoman, and radio personality finally feels she has something to say. Over the past ten years, more than 300 short stories about life and love have surfaced. As writer and storyteller, she has let the power of her gentle words touch the hearts and souls of her readers and listeners. (715) 532-7292. <jannusch@mscfs.edu>

PEGGY KLINE is the proud mother of Melissa, Angela, and Trevor, who have provided her with much joy (and material)! She is a nationally known speaker and humorist who specializes in nurturing the needs of women with humor and hope. Her award-winning program, *Who's Mothering Mom?*, has been sponsored by Gerber Products company for over five years and has delighted moms across this nation. Her ability to reach and inspire women everywhere has found her on national talk-show radio and in newspapers across the country. She can touch and tickle the hearts of women at your next women's conference or event. (616) 891-1153.

PATRICIA KULZER is a mother and administrative assistant. She is currently channeling her artistic energies into administrating a family-based business creating heirloom memory quilts. (630) 257-2086.

CATHERINE LANIGAN has been writing for twenty years and is the author of twenty-one novels, including the novelizations of *Romancing the Stone* and *The Jewel of the Nile*. She has introduced a new breed of heroine into the literary fold, "The Evolving Woman," a character who builds an arsenal of wisdom, dignity, and courage that will fortify her capacity to love and be loved despite very real tragedies and crises. Her self-empowerment stems from an abiding spiritual faith, which guides her and continually renews hope. Look for her recent release, *In Love's Shadow,* and her upcoming release, *The Legend Makers,* to be published in July 1999 by MIRA Books. www.clanigan.com

MARY LoVERDE, M.S., A.N.P., is a professional speaker and founder of Life Balance, Inc. Her passion is researching new ways to balance career success with a happy and healthy family. She is the author of *Stop Screaming at the Microwave: How to Connect Your Disconnected Life,* published by Fireside / Simon & Schuster, and she has been seen on *Oprah.* She has produced an audiotape series entitled *June Cleaver Never Fried Bacon in a Bill Blass Dress.* For information about her customized Memory Jar and Memory Cards, please call (303) 755-5806.

JOANNE McCALL, a veteran radio broadcaster for eighteen years, is cohost of a weekly radio talk show in Portland, Oregon. As president of McCall Public Relations, Joanne counts one of her greatest passions as helping authors and speakers promote their work. She considers working on the *Chocolate* series with Kay Allenbaugh and the contributing authors to be an honor. Joanne leads a joyful life with her husband, Gary, their dog, Houston, and cats, Thelma and Louise. (503) 245-3107.

JUDITH McCLURE is the director and resident minister of the Center for Expanding Consciousness in Phoenix, Arizona. She, along with her dog Bear and cat Angel, is the official welcoming committee for Sunday services and the many classes held at the center. She teaches "Speaking and Creating with Your Angels" and "Making Unique Water Fountains for Your Spiritual Garden." (602) 279-3998. <j_mcclure@earthlink.net>

CAROLYN MASTERS, M.S., Ed.S.P., is the president of Masters Resource Group. She consults, writes, and speaks on the human side of change. She is the author of *When Change Is Your*

Company's Middle Name, a handbook for executives and business owners experiencing company transition. She holds a masters' degree in guidance and counseling and an education-specialist degree in administration. She is a member of the National Speakers Association and the Arizona Speakers Association. She, her husband, and their miniature dachshund enjoy their Southwest living in Tucson. (520) 297-6674. <Ckmasters@aol.com>

MARGUERITE MURER is a professional speaker, an educator, and the executive assistant to the president of the Texas Rangers Baseball Club. Combining her educational background with her unique baseball experiences, Marguerite inspires and energizes her audiences to step up to the plate and hit a home run. (817) 273-5234.

LINDA NASH, M.B.A., is a nationally known speaker and career coach and the author of *Surviving in the Jungle* and *The Shorter Road to Success.* Her practical techniques, enthusiasm, humor, great stories, and motivational style inspire her audiences. She speaks to companies, associations, and organizations on change, communication, personal growth, and career. An ordained interfaith minister, she speaks to church groups and offers spiritual retreats for women. For information on Linda's speaking services, retreats, books, new career workbook, and tape series, *Becoming the Real You and Getting Paid for It,* call (800) 701-9782. <Lindaljn@aol.com>

SARAH NEWBY is a native New Yorker, a wife, and a mother of six. Her professional training was as an executive secretary, and she spent the last twenty-five years working with her husband in their elevator consulting business. "In a Mother's Absence" is her first submission for publication, and she was thrilled to have it accepted. She wants to complete the novel she has always dreamed of writing.

MARTHA E. NICHOLSON is a special-needs educator in the field of learning disabilities. She is working on her first book, *I Want a Room with a Window*, a recounting of her misadventures at an elementary school. She provides testing and private tutoring to learning-disabled children and adults. She is also active in crafts and quilting. (978) 343-2939.

MAUREEN NUNN is the creator and host of a nationally syndicated and award-winning cable television series, *Everyday Heroes*, on how ordinary people can change the world, airing twice weekly on Kaleidoscope. Bilingual, she also hosts a weekly Spanish call-in show with Lety Dominguez Bolivar and explores issues in the lives of Hispanics today. The show, "Comunidad Latina con Maria y Lety," has earned three Diamond Awards and a President's Award. She has produced videos about pediatric AIDS, children and cancer, and the impact of leukemia. She earned the American Cancer Society's National Honor Citation and has received the prestigious CableACE Award. (310) 544-3260.

O. C. O'CONNELL is a freelance writer and editor who celebrates the passing of every "snack day" as a culinary triumph. She resides with her beloved and their twin angel girls in a perpetual state of passion, chaos, and negotiation. She was a ghost writer for Intel Corporation on the book *The PC Dads' Guide to Raising a Computer Smart Family*. Her work has also been featured in *Chocolate for a Woman's Heart*, *Twins* magazine, *The Journal of Case Management*, and *The AORN Journal*. (303) 730-6745. <ococonnell@att.net>

REV. MARY OMWAKE has been the senior minister of Unity Church of Overland Park in Kansas since 1989. Under her leadership, the congregation has grown from under 200 to 2,450 members. She is a founding member of the Association for Global New Thought, and is committed to supporting authentic spiritual growth and rendering genuine service to an awakening world. (913) 649-1750.

KATHY ADATTE OTT lives in Saginaw, Michigan. After her son Timothy's death, she returned to college and earned a B.A. in communications. Currently, she is very thankful to be a stay-at-home mom while raising Christopher (nine years) and Katherine (five years). She is in the process of writing her first book, *A Glorious Triumph: A Glimpse into Becoming a Mother Through Foreign Adoption*. (517) 792-6738. <Adatte425@aol.com>

DEBBIE PETRICEK, M.S., N.L.P., is founder of In Potentia: The Center for Creativity and Development, in Portland, Oregon. With passions for psychology, art, and communication, she promotes the importance of creativity in culture, and positive imagery in health and wellness. Her center provides a playful and productive forum that fosters creative expression, learning, and development. Those whom she coaches build skills that become invaluable as they continue to change and grow. (503) 226-9161.

LILLIAN QUASCHNICK is a former foreign-language teacher. Humor is her favorite kind of writing, and she is currently writing about her experience as a first-generation Italian-American. She is also collaborating on a book about the raisin industry. (209) 843-2524.

LINDA RAY is a hospice nurse and freelance writer who has, through necessity and sometimes choice, lived in fifteen states. Many years ago, she decided to bloom where she was planted and avoid the shrinking-violet phenomenon of being uprooted. She has now "retired" to a forested area of her home state of Oregon where mail is delivered three days a week. She pursues love, outdoor life, and writing. <rlbrning@jeffnet.org>

JOAN ROELKE is a former banking executive and freelance writer. She lives at Lake Tahoe, where she is currently working on her second novel. (530) 581-0662.

JOYCE M. SALTMAN, Ed.D., has been a professor of special education at Southern Connecticut State University since 1975. She also teaches graduate courses called "The Enhancement of Learning Through Humor" every semester, as well as at a graduate Institute called HELP: Healing, Education, Laughter and Play. To lighten people up, in her spare time she travels throughout the world giving a hundred lectures a year called "Laughter: Rx for Survival" and "Dealing with Difficult People." (203) 272-9519.

MARY SASS, who has an M.A. in counseling, is a writer, artist, lecturer, and former teacher who has published many essays, short stories, and articles about writing. She has won awards for her radio scripts and television documentaries, as well as her oil paintings. She has written novels and illustrated a Christmas novella, *The Katy Ornament*. A member of Mystery Writers of America and the MWA Speakers' Bureau, she is listed in *Who's Who of American Women*, *Who's Who of the Midwest*, and *Who's Who in Entertainment*. (847) 674-7118, and (616) 432-4466, June to September.

ANNE SPOLLEN, with an M.A. in English literature, is certified to teach Spanish and English, which she has taught at just about every level from seventh grade through college. She writes poetry and fiction, has been published in numerous literary journals, and in 1998 received a Pushcart nomination for fiction. She still "perceives" the unspoken about Christopher and Philip and is hoping for the same for her newborn daughter, Emma. <shawangunks@msn.com>

LYNNE SWARTZLANDER is a businesswoman, writer, and speaker who uses humor ("I found out recently that Superwoman doesn't live at my address. I'm still stunned!") and insight to encourage others on life's journey. Her love for people and animals and her passion to be a positive influence in an often negative world keep her looking for new and often humorous ways to cope with modern life. (360) 574-8055. <ohnomocha@aol.com>

SUSIE TROCCOLO has recently moved from owning a consulting business in a high-tech industry to a new hybrid life. These days she works two days a week from a home office, two days a week in her organic vegetable garden, and one day a week doing volunteer work with children. Swearing off girl shoes and pantyhose, she now walks Rufus and Sassy rain or shine in Portland, Oregon. To celebrate growing older, joy, and change, she has just written a book entitled *Growing Down Stories* as a gift for family and friends. <Auguri@ix.netcom.com>

MICHELE WALLACE-CAMPANELLI, novelist, is a Brevard County resident and author of *Hero of Her Heart*, published by Blue Note Books. She has also been a guest columnist for *Florida Today* newspaper. Her commentary about Harry Caray brought her acclaim, including a personal thank you letter from the Chicago Cubs' Chip Caray. *Keeper of the Shroud* and *Margarita*, her latest manuscripts, have just been completed and currently are in the editing process. www.netcom.com/~wallace3 <mswallace@juno.com>

PATRICIA WILSON is the author of the bestselling audiotape series *Living in Excellence*, and of eight inspirational books. *How Can I Be Over the Hill When I Haven't Reached the Top Yet?* and *Why Pray When You Can Take Pills and Worry: A Frazzled Mother's Guide to Raising Teens* continue to be ongoing favorites with her readers.

She is an international speaker and workshop leader, best known for her down-to-earth style and humorous anecdotes, which have charmed audiences from Manila to London, and from Seattle to New York. She lives on a small island off the Atlantic coast in Nova Scotia, Canada. (902) 885-3193. <http://www.deeperwaters.com>

TONI WOOD is a writer, volunteer, and mother who lives in the Kansas City area with her husband and three lively boys, Alex, Grant, and Nicholas. She is a former reporter for the *Kansas City Star*, and her articles and essays have appeared in many magazines, newspapers, and books. She has shared her interest in art and different cultures with children at church and school. (913) 441-0659. <toniwrites@aol.com>

LYNNE LAYTON ZIELINSKI exuberantly enjoys the friendship of her seven adult children, the magical inspiration of thirteen grandkids, and the loving partnership of her husband of forty-one years. Formerly a nurse, now a business owner, and always a people watcher, Lynne believes life is a gift from God and that what we do with it is our gift to God. She writes accordingly. Phone: (205) 880-9052. <Excel 11047@aol.com>

ACKNOWLEDGMENTS

A heartfelt thank you goes to the *Chocolate for a Mother's Heart* storytelling moms and children of moms for the messages they've shared. The positive ripple effect from their words will spread throughout the world. Their ability to put into story form the hilarious, touching, soul-searching, poignant moments they've experienced is what creates the rich variety inside the pages of this book.

My continued appreciation goes to my agent, Peter Miller, for his energetic, professional expertise and to the "Chocolate" ladies on his staff—Delin Cormeny and Allison Wolcott—for their ongoing support. Major kudos goes to my executive editor, Becky Cabaza. And many, many thanks to her assistant, Carrie Thornton; my publicist, Helen Adams; and marketing and publicity gurus vice presidents Christine Lloreda and Sue Fleming Holland, along with the rest of the team at Fireside/Simon & Schuster who all have become "Chocolate" moms!

A very special thanks to Burky Achilles and Ellen Hiltebrand for their editing expertise, and Carol Zavodsky for her office support.

As always, my undying love and appreciation to the memory of my mom. Her essence permeates the tone of *Chocolate for a Mother's Heart.*

MORE CHOCOLATE STORIES?

Do you have a short story you want published that fits the spirit of *Chocolate for a Mother's Heart* or *Chocolate for a Woman's Soul?* I am planning, using a similar format, future editions that will feature love, divine moments, overcoming obstacles, following our intuition, and humorous events that teach us to laugh at ourselves. I am seeking heartwarming stories of one to four pages in length that feed and lift the spirit and encourage us to go for our dreams.

I invite you to join me in these future projects by sending your special story for consideration. If your story is selected, you will be listed as a contributing author, and you can include a biographical paragraph of your choice. For more information, or to send a story, please contact:

Kay Allenbaugh
P. O. Box 2165
Lake Oswego, OR 97035

For more information, please visit my Web site!
http://www.chocolateforwomen.com

ABOUT THE AUTHOR

Kay Allenbaugh is the author of *Chocolate for a Woman's Soul*, *Chocolate for a Woman's Heart*, *Chocolate for a Woman's Heart and Soul*, and *Chocolate for a Lover's Heart* and resides with her husband, Eric Allenbaugh (author of *Wake-Up Calls: You Don't Have to Sleepwalk Through Your Life, Love or Career!*) in Lake Oswego, Oregon.

Don't Miss the First Three Volumes of Delicious

Chocolate

Stories

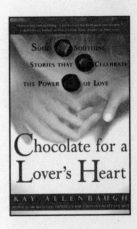

Chocolate for a Woman's Soul
0-684-83217-8, $12.00

Chocolate for a Woman's Heart
0-684-84896-1, $11.00

Chocolate for a Lover's Heart
0-684-86298-0, $11.00

Also available from
Simon & Schuster Audio
0-671-57964-9, $16.00

Also available from
Simon & Schuster Audio
0-671-58223-2, $16.00

F FIRESIDE
A Division of Simon & Schuster
A VIACOM COMPANY
www.SimonSays.com